Clergy Table Talk

Eavesdropping on Ministry Issues
in the 21st Century

Kent Ira Groff

Energion Publications
Gonzalez, Florida
www.energionpubs.com

2012
Academy of Parish Clergy Conversations in Ministry - 1

Cover Design: Nick May

ISBN10: 1-893729-11-7
ISBN13: 978-1893729-11-7
Library of Congress Control Number: 2012937390

Table of Contents

Spiritual Practices

SERIES PREFACE

Parish ministry can be an exciting and challenging vocation. This has always been the case, but it is perhaps even truer today. At least in the European and North American contexts, institutional forms of religion are finding themselves pushed to the sidelines. Their purpose and value has been questioned, and with these questions come further questions about the professional status of those who are called to serve these congregations.

A generation ago, congregational ministers might see themselves as members of a professional class, similar to that of medical doctors and attorneys. The Academy of Parish Clergy, the sponsor of this book series, was founded with just that vision – to encourage and enhance the professional practice of parish ministry. This was to be accomplished by setting professional standards, including the encouragement to engage in regular continuing education, and then providing a means of accountability to those standards. Although the broader culture has raised questions about the professional standing of parish clergy, the need for professional standards, continuing education, and accountability remains as important today as ever before. This is because the world in which ministry is being done is ever changing, and therefore clergy must adapt, learn new skills, and reposition themselves for a new day. It is helpful, therefore, to walk in the company of others who are also engaged in similar kinds of ministry.

What makes parish ministry both exciting and challenging is that most clergy are generalists. They're like the family practioner, dealing with a wide variety of issues and people. No day is exactly the same, for they serve as teachers, preachers, worship leaders, providers of pastoral care, administrators, and social justice leaders. They may be more gifted in some areas than others, but ultimately they find themselves engaged in a wide variety of tasks that often push them to the limits of ability and endurance. It is not a vocation that can be undertaken on one's own, and for a variety of reasons parish ministers need to find a community of others who share this calling, so that they might find encouragement, support, and ideas for dealing with parish life and ministry in the broader world.

Part of the founding vision of the Academy of Parish Clergy was to facilitate this need to find a community of peers, and with this in mind Academy members were encouraged to create and join together in Colleague Groups, where they could encourage one another and explore issues that confront clergy in their daily ministry, often using the "Case Study Method," which was emerging at the time among the professions. That model is still available, but it is the hope of the editors of this series that these books will also provide a foundation for conversation in clergy groups.

This vision continues to sustain the Academy more than forty years after its founding, and the new APC book series, *Conversations in Ministry*, seeks to extend this vision by offering to clergy books written primarily by practicing clergy for practicing clergy dealing with the issues that confront them in ministry today. Each book, published in partnership with Energion Publications, will be brief and focused (under 100 pages). Each book is designed to encourage reflection and conversation among clergy. The editors and authors of these books hope that the books will be taken up by groups of clergy and inspire conversation.

It is important to point out the use of the preposition "in." The conversations that are envisioned here are not simply about ministry, but are designed to emerge from within the context of ministry. Although the initial book covers a variety of issues facing clergy, future books will focus on specific issues including clergy ethics, self-care, preaching, worship leadership, congregational administration, use of social media. Each book will include discussion questions that can aid group conversation, but also individual reflection. Each book will reflect the purpose of the series, but each author will take the conversation in the direction the topic suggests.

May this series of books be a blessing to all who read them.

Robert D. Cornwall, APC
General Editor

Orientation

"The barrier that gets in the way of ministering is ministry," a seasoned pastor told a retreat group I was leading. From serving as a parish pastor for two decades, and longer still as a retreat leader, seminary professor, and spiritual guide for ministers and other servants, I've heard clergy talk about myriad issues that initially seem like distractions: congregational conflict, administration overload, denominational politics, pressure to say what folks want to hear—physical, spiritual, and emotional burnout.

Would it seem like a miracle if such barriers could become bridges to deepening spiritual life and vocation? I invite you to ponder: When in your life has a ministry emergency morphed into an occasion for spiritual emergence?

Ways to use *Clergy Table Talk* are countless. It's interactive, with questions in the text and at the end of each chapter, along with Spiritual Practices that can enrich any way you read it:

√   For personal and spiritual formation and daily devotions;
√   For nurturing a spiritual friendship with one other minister;
√   For an existing or a new clergy colleague group;
√   For a short-term lay adult class with a pastor sitting in;
√   For lay ministers and church staff members;
√   For students interested in ministry.

At the end of each chapter, I include a *spiritual practice* inviting you to integrate the chapter's theme into contemplative and active life. These resources lend themselves for personal reflection or for use as an opening meditation for a committee meeting or a clergy gathering. Each Spiritual Practice is followed by *questions* for personal reflection or for group conversation—in person, by texting, Internet, or phone.

My goal is to offer a variety of ways to explore spiritual insights from within yourself and from others in a friendship or group. The three Resources in the back offer an invitation to deepen your personal spiritual life through the practice of keeping a journal, to expand your communal spiritual life through a colleague group, and to focus your ministry through a life mission statement.

All of these—fifteen reflections on lively issues along with spiritual practices, the questions and resources for growth—call us to the roots of ministry in God's grace. This is what the Academy of Parish Clergy is all about. As a member from the Academy's initial founding, I want to acknowledge with thanks the integration of intellectual, professional, and spiritual growth opportunities the APC provides.

The inauguration of this book series offers yet another venue for deepening personal spiritual practices and broadening professional practices with colleagues in ministry, grounded in the Source of light and life.

1

Crisis of Awareness: A Barebones Spiritual Practice

Life must be lived forwards, but it can only be understood backwards.

—Søren Kierkegaard

Late one afternoon, I-70 north of Denver was one gigantic stop-and-go parking lot when it happened—kaboom! In a nanosecond of inattentiveness I failed to notice the car in front of me had stopped. Failure to examine what's going on around us causes most accidents.

Failure to examine evidence can be a life-and-death matter. Timothy Cole spent twenty-four years in a Texas prison where he died of asthma in 1999, wrongly convicted of rape by judge and jury without a shred of physical evidence. Ten years later, in February 2009, an Austin court acquitted Cole posthumously. The victim confessed she had identified the wrong person. Human acts of injustice happen because someone is blind-sided.

We get blind-sided in a myriad ways. He has a "silent" heart attack in his fifties. She doesn't see the church conflict brewing till it blows up in her fourth year.

Turning aside to see. We can't deal with any issues in ministry realistically or creatively unless we stay awake. Awareness is the beginning, middle and end of the spiritual life. A rabbi friend tells me that the burning bush was not the real miracle, but rather that Moses "turned aside to see" (Exodus 3:3-4). The Hebrew word *shema* means hear, listen, or pay attention.

Life is ultimately defined by what we pay attention to. What we focus on feeds us—my translation of Ludwig Feuerbach's idea that "man is what he eats." Genuine spirituality doesn't just focus on sweetness and light, but also finds grist for growth by reflecting on struggles, diminishments, wrong turns.

"Experience is the best teacher," people say. But as friends in Alcoholics Anonymous are quick to tell me, you can cycle through the same experience over and over, and never learn from it. So I've tweaked the saying: "Experience reflected upon is the real teacher."

Practicing recollection. In anything basic, like breathing or swimming, we need the oscillating rhythm that Søren Kierkegaard describes: "Life must be lived forwards, but it can only be understood backwards."[1] It's the best reason I know for practicing examen and for keeping a spiritual journal (see Resource One).

Sankofa, a primal symbol from West Africa, provides a graphic expression of Kierkegaard's thought. *Sankofa* portrays a bird with its feet facing forward and its head looking back, usually with an egg in its mouth. It reminds us to keep an eye on our past, to draw from its precious treasures, while moving forward into the future.[2] "Go back and fetch it" is a good translation, echoing Socrates' words about the examined life.

Picture this little bird joyously dancing its way through life—feet forwards, eyes backwards, sideways, head forwards again! Go back and fetch the essence of life.

By practicing recollection, you harvest the essence of life while moving forward on this swiftly tilting planet. Imagine yourself hearing this bird sing in your heart: *If I hadn't gone through that struggle then, I wouldn't be prepared for this struggle now.*

A daily examen provides a frame for balancing the active contemplative life. Notice the *gifts* and *struggles* in the daily grit (retroactive grace). Then ask, in light of what's going on, what's the *invitation* (proactive grace)? How is Life or God inviting me to move forward? Sometimes the invitation is to find the gift in the struggle.[3]

Let this story offer a different slant. A pastor had just returned from vacation when he met with me for spiritual companioning. He began putting himself down. "I haven't written in my journal for months, I'm snapping at my wife, I'm not exercising—look at this roll," he said with hands on his belly. I recall pausing, and then a simple question came to me: "Nick, what do you think God might want to say to you?" He grew quiet, put his head in his hands, and then groped for words. "I ... I think ... maybe ... God might be saying, 'Try to remember what you already know.'" "Wow," I said as we both sat in awe. Then both of us reached for our journals to record the gem.

"Try to remember what you already know" is the best reason I can think of for constantly reviewing your life, in times of crisis or calm, to look back by looking within your own experiences to tap inner wisdom, unique to the pattern of your faith journey, to guide you through the next obstacle on your path. The Resident Expert on your life lives in you.

Socrates put it well: "The unexamined life is not worth living." And if that's true, then we need a corollary: "The examined life is worth living twice."

SPIRITUAL PRACTICE 1: AN EXAMEN OF AWARENESS

Here is a simple exercise for scanning over the horizon of your conscious awareness at the beginning or end of the day.

Invite the One who is the Light of the world to walk with you, scanning over the past twenty-four hours (or recent period) ... Gently sift through events and encounters. Breathe deeply: in ... out ... Imagine things unfolding as from a slow moving train...

1. **Gift (Wow!)** Give thanks for any gift(s) of the day. Celebrate God's empowering love at a time or times when you felt loved or loving.

2. **Struggle (Whoa.)** Notice times when you struggled to feel loved, or loving, some unrest in your soul, some unresolved tension. Celebrate God's undefeated love and hear: "You are my beloved."

3. **Invitation (What now?)** Ask God, What grace do I need to name and claim to be more whole today? Pause... Allow a word or phrase—an image or metaphor—to come to mind. Begin to repeat it, slowly with your breathing; or picture it if it's an image. (Silence)

Last: Imagine a mini-hidden video at home or work: Visualize yourself acting out of this new grace, as if you are already whole. Return to active life using a line of a poem, scripture or song. You might make some notes in your journal.

For a group: Leader may read the examen aloud, prayerfully. Afterward, invite each person to share with one other, in dyads (2-3 minutes each). Afterward, the leader may invite each dyad to conclude with a brief silent prayer for each other. Then go to questions 1-5.

(Kent Ira Groff, adapted from *Facing East, Praying West,* based on *The Spiritual Exercises* of Ignatius of Loyola.)

FOR PERSONAL REFLECTION OR GROUP CONVERSATION

1. Engage in the examen exercise, personally or as a group (see **"for a group"** above). What new edges or perspectives did this exercise open up for you?

2. What spiritual practices help you to cultivate attentiveness?

3. How might you incorporate this simple form of prayer into the beginning or end of your day? How might you practice it informally throughout the day? With a group at the end of a committee meeting?

4. How might you use this as a tool for keeping a spiritual journal? (See Resource One.)

2
Loss of Soul:
A Crisis of Integrity,
Passion and Wholeness

If the spirit within us withers, so too will all the world we build about us.

—Theodore Roszak

I had just met with Dana, who, after preaching a sermon and upon arriving at the door to greet the congregation, had a flash thought: *If I weren't a pastor, I wouldn't go to church.*

A crisis of integrity. Clergy often live with a gnawing duplicity, a crisis in integrity. On a deeper level, it's a crisis of the soul. Theodore Roszak, pioneer in eco-psychology, said prophetically: "We can now recognize that the fate of the soul is the fate of the social order; that if the spirit within us withers, so too will all the world we build about us."

There are lots of reasons for this crisis. Spiritual seekers and leaders read John Dominic Crossan and Marcus Borg and don't know what to believe about the Jesus they thought they knew (see Chapter 14). People in the pew feel bewildered, while many clergy feel stuck. "Faithless Faith Worker" reads ethicist Randy Cohen's column in *The New York Times Magazine*, about a clergyperson who is now an atheist. But what else is a pastor trained to do?

"I'm here on this retreat because I can't worship while I lead worship," said a pastor. I affirm the need for retreat, but the comment makes me sad.

How can we who plan and lead worship invite others into "the holy of holies" if we are not standing on holy ground ourselves?

And if spiritual leaders cannot sense the Presence in worship, which exists for the very purpose of experiencing God, how less likely when we go about the mundane administration of programs?

The new crisis I am seeing is this: *that ministry itself is getting in the way of re-presenting Christ in the world.* I found this saddening when I said it in *The Soul of Tomorrow's Church*. Now, a dozen years later, I find it frightening.

The soul of ministry. Here is a desperate call to restore the s*oul* of ministry. When I speak of *soul*, I'm lifting up three positive qualities corresponding to serious needs of congregations and spiritual leaders in Western culture.

Integrity. When one hears the phrase "selling your soul," it conveys the sense of expediency: "I owe my soul to the company store." This crisis in integrity is illustrated when we lead worship but do not worship, or talk of love while belittling others. The soul of ministry is about practicing what we teach (Matthew 23:3). It's about spiritual integrity: how can today's leaders embody their being in God in our doing in the world?

Passion. "She did it with all her heart and soul" means to do something with passion. Seekers and leaders confess that religious life is often boring, lacking energy, like salt that has lost its taste. It is lukewarm—neither cold nor hot. In words reminiscent of Kierkegaard, the age will die not from sin, but from lack of passion. But passion also means suffering. For Christian leaders, to rediscover the passion of Christ in the structural life of the church will be painful, as old wineskins burst on the way to restoring the integrity and energy of soul.

Wholeness. "'Tis all in pieces, all coherence gone,' wrote the poet John Donne. Ministry in an overspecialized world gets complicated and fragmented. The s*oul* of ministry is about healing personal *and* social fragmentation, finding simplicity in a multiplicity of stimuli. As W. E. B. Du Bois says in *The Souls of Black Folk*, soul involves a totality of life's suffering and joy. Soul is a synonym for life; the word *nefesh* in Hebrew speaks of integration of one's whole being:

"Bless the Lord, O my soul, and all that is within me, bless God's holy name" (Psalm 103:1).

God's call today is for the believing community and its leaders to make present these three qualities—the integrity, passion, and wholeness of God's love in the world. It is to lead these incredible fragile communities by our presence to embody their mission. Some three decades ago, former AT&T executive, Robert Greenleaf, spoke prophetically in *Servant Leadership*:

> Most charitable institutions, of which the church is one, have tended to view the problems of society as "out there," and it was assumed that service to the "out there" was the sole justification for their existence. Now the view is emerging that one begins "in here," inside the serving institution, and makes of *it* a model institution. This model, *because it is a thing of beauty, in itself,* becomes a powerful serving force.[4]

Communities of faith yearn for this miracle: to become "a powerful serving force" even while experiencing turbulent changes in personal and corporate life. Can clergy be "the still point in the turning world"—in a dance of change and tradition?

Six practices. Here are six ingredients that we can practice over time to restore our burned-out souls and infuse a healthy spirituality in our relationships and ministry.

1. Engaging in honest-to-God, holistic Spiritual Practices that nurture one's own soul in community and in solitude;
2. Balancing one's schedule with sabbath and service, speech and silence, ministry and home life;
3. Spiritual mentoring/direction and healthy friendships with appropriate boundaries;
4. Transforming failure by mining gifts in weaknesses and strengths;

5. Integrating the mystical, political, intellectual and physical arenas;
6. A life mission linking one's unique passion with a focused aspect of the world's need.

These are ways to practice holistic spirituality. "What is spirituality?" a student rushed up to me and asked, two minutes before my class would begin. I gave the question to the class, and here's the definition that emerged: *Spirituality is learning to respond rather than react to events of the world and circumstances of one's life, in a manner that blesses the world and one's own soul.* Could this be what Plato meant by "the education of desire"—that every manner of thing be transformed for good?

Wherever inklings of such transformation happen—in a fleeting moment of worship, in a painful glimpse of self in public, in the ecstasy of a child's insight, in a self-forgetting act of altruism—we have tasted joy in sacrifice; we experience Eucharist.

Such moments of genuine worship are at once moments when the mind is renewed while at the same time extending hospitality—even if it is to the stranger within oneself.

SPIRITUAL PRACTICE 2: CENTERING PRAYER AS CONTEMPLATIVE PRACTICE

Meditate on your real desire or yearning beneath all the doing of ministry. Allow a simple word to arise, one that seems to sum up that deep longing. Examples: Love, Peace, Trust; or a short phrase of scripture such as "Be still, and know ..." (Psalm 46:10)—or just "Be ..." For some a word in another language helps avoid thinking: *Amor* (love); *Shalom* or *Salaam* (peace in Hebrew and Arabic); *Maranatha* (Our Lord come in Aramaic). Or a visual image or metaphor may arise. Begin repeating it, gently, in rhythm to your breathing ... Or visualizing it ... Then let go of the word or image: simply allow yourself to be present, loving and being loved. (Try using this method to cultivate 15-20 minutes of silence daily.) Log reflections in your journal.

QUESTIONS FOR PERSONAL OR GROUP REFLECTION:

1. "The first service that one renders to the community is that of listening to one's brother and sister," wrote Dietrich Bonhoeffer in *Life Together.* How does the practice of listening with God in contemplative prayer assist contemplative listening with our neighbor?

2. "Spirituality is learning to respond rather than react to events of the world and circumstances of one's life, in a manner that blesses the world and one's own soul." In what ways is spirituality "learning ...?" How does "react" sound different from "respond"? How to you strike the balance in blessing the world and your own soul?

3

Restoring the Soul: Nine Lenses for Holistic Spirituality

The Lord is my shepherd, I shall not want:
who makes me lie down in green pastures,
who leads me beside the still waters,
who restores my soul.
—Psalm 23:1-2, AT

What do folks mean when they talk about *soul?* It seems so nebulous. Spirituality often gets a bum rap for seeming disconnected from the stuff of life. Yet the Hebrew *Shema* is a call to live and love awake with all our senses: "Hear, O Israel: The Lord is our God, the Lord alone. You shall love the Lord your God with all your heart, and the all your soul, and with all your mind, and with all your strength," quotes Rabbi Jesus from the Torah (Matthew 22:37-38; Deuteronomy 6:4-5). *Shema* means hear, listen, pay attention, wake up, or contemplate. It's a call to holistic spirituality.

A paradigm for holistic ministry. "Love your neighbor as yourself," the second command (Matthew 22:39; Leviticus 19:18), flows from the first. Contemplating divine love promotes contemplating our neighbor's needs. Serving others is a direct outflow of a holistic, loving experiential relationship with God. If we practice embodied spirituality that nurtures one's whole self and soul, then loving neighbor will incorporate embodied dimensions. Holistic ministry is the fruit of holistic spirituality.

What would it look like to live and love with *soul?* The "multiple intelligences," pioneered by Howard Gardner, offer nine lenses to restore the soul in all of life, adaptable for varied personality types, learning styles, culture, and gender contexts. Some modes are highly developed in a person, others less, yet everyone has some aptitude in each.

1. *Linguistic/verbal*: As a child can't thrive isolated from speech, so the spiritual journeyer needs a community of other colleagues to learn the language of love.

2. *Logical/mathematical*: Theo*logical* learning is reflection on the *experience* of the Holy—theology is "faith seeking understanding" (Anselm of Canterbury).

3. *Spatial/visual*: Spatial learning arranges a room, explores geography, plans cross-cultural events, honors holy places and creates inner space and fantasy.

4. *Musical/rhythmic*: "One who sings prays twice." Singing, drumming or piping your troubles makes the blues beautiful and celebrates life's rhythms.

5. *Kinesthetic/bodily*: Gestures begin a symphony, turn a baseball game upside down, and express the soul: bowing, kneeling, dancing; handcrafting, playing.

6. *Interpersonal*: Extroverts tend to encounter the Sacred in community, introverts in small groups or one-to-one, yet both need relationships.

7. *Intrapersonal*: Most neglected in technological society, solitude and silence are an introvert's joy and preserve the extrovert's sanity; it taps internal wisdom.

8. *Naturalist*: The Sacred is revealed through the book of nature (as well as sacred books), its awe and beauty, its patterns of devastation and renewal.

9. *Existentialist.* Here's the "why, why" of a two-year-old or an Einstein. Artists, mystics, scientists and philosophers ask questions that lead to more mystery.

Creative story is one way to participate in elements of all nine: witness operas, musicals, ballads, dramas; stories involve kinesthetic, linear and visual modes. These approaches are so usable because they allow the Word of love to become flesh in every sphere of life.

Spiritual and *emotional* intelligence inhabit all nine. Some have criticized Gardner for having no separate spiritual or emotional categories, yet such a separation would fly in the face of embodied, holistic spirituality. Archimedes ran naked out of his bath when a new scientific truth struck him, shouting, *Eureka!*—"I've found it!" Pascal encountered the mystic Christ via mathematical calculations; John Denver sang about nature's "Rocky Mountain High." Psalms are full of kinesthetic gestures: climbing, bowing, kneeling; folding, clapping and lifting hands. "Bless the Lord, O my soul, and *all* that is within me bless God's holy name!" (Psalm 103:1, AT).

For centuries René Descartes' maxim "I think, therefore I am" has skewed modern culture toward printed, logical, theological and technological intelligence. But if you examine only what you "think" you believe you can "feel" like a spiritual flunky. Actually you may "know" the Holy in your experience, in your gut, your heart—your primal brain. Today's spiritual quest is pri-modern: to link our primal knowing with modern knowledge.

These nine perspectives are so liberating because they are so healing. The tendency of Western educational and religious systems toward linguistic and logical modes cramps the souls of many genuine God-seekers and spiritual leaders. "The same shoe doesn't fit every foot," and these nine lenses open up vistas to find and follow the Lord of life in our lived experience. They invite us to learn to yearn always, and all ways.

We can get too comfortable with the often-quoted wisdom, "Pray as you can, and not as you can't." So consider an addendum to stretch the soul, "Until I try some ways I think I can't pray, I don't know quite so well how I can."

SPIRITUAL PRACTICE 3: EXPANDING PERSONAL PRAYER

Glance over the nine multiple learning modes. Now review your personal Spiritual Practices. Notice one of two of the nine modes that are least present in your prayer life. Challenge yourself to choose a couple that stretch your normal pattern. For example, if most of your prayers are verbal, you might ask how you might develop intrapersonal practices (silence, centering prayer) or kinesthetic practices (gestures such as kneeling, stretching, dancing; tensing and releasing hands). Group context: invite group members to share one-to-one, then as a whole group.

QUESTIONS FOR PERSONAL OR GROUP REFLECTION:

1. What would it look like to incorporate these nine more in your personal life?
2. What would it look like to incorporate these more in your communal worship life?
3. What would it look like to incorporate these more in groups and committees?
4. What would it look like to incorporate these more in informal conversations, counseling and family settings?

4

Honoring Your Temple: Praying with the Body

The body takes the shape of the soul.

—Anonymous Mystic

Etched in my mind is the hunched figure of a six-foot-six pastor and scholar, silhouetted in a hallway in late afternoon's sun. I thought of the ancient wisdom, "The body takes the shape of the soul." Exchanging greetings, we entered my office to meet for the first time.

We conversed for a while. Then we sat for a bit in silence. I sensed his discouragement. Soon he drifted into talking about tiredness, the value of "shutting down the computers"—being instead of doing. At some point I found myself asking: "What is sabbath for you?"

"Well, reading," he said, "but I haven't been reading much. Taking my boat on the river, but I don't take time. Walking with my wife, but I get home late at night. And music."

"Oh?" I queried.

"A bit of piano. And the trumpet—I used to play with my family, but my lip isn't even in shape anymore."

A year and many experiences later, my friend received an award from his alma mater for "excellence in ministry." The night of the awards banquet he was standing tall. Afterward I met his wife, who began telling me how one evening she had come home from teaching in a nearby college. "And when I heard the trumpet, I knew something was changing in my husband."

Embodied spirituality. You can see in this story the interplay between verbal, logical, kinesthetic, visual, musical, interpersonal, intrapersonal, naturalist and existentialist modes of spiritual experience. One of the big barriers to deepening the spiritual life is the artificial body vs. soul split. Despite exceptions to the contrary, ascetic disciplines are meant to enhance the whole person including the body, not degrade it.

In Jewish and Christian tradition the idea of "resurrection of the body" is a bold affirmation that new life in the Spirit blesses the whole person—right here in this world. The apostle Paul insists the body is a "temple of the Holy Spirit" (1 Corinthians 6:19). Likewise Basava, a 12th century Hindu reformer, reflects on the body as a sacred temple:

> The rich will make temples for Siva:
> What shall I, a poor man, do?
> My legs are pillars, the body is a shrine,
> The head is the cupola, of gold.[5]

If we *really* listened to these temple-bodies of ours, how might we hear echoes of the lost liturgies of our lives?

Your body's rhythms as prayer. The *Shema* bids us to love God "with all our might"—in Hebrew meaning the intensity of our whole being. When the apostle Paul urges believers "to present your bodies… to God, which is your spiritual worship," it includes the mind: "that you may be transformed by the renewing of your minds, so that you may discern what is the will of God" (Romans 12:1-2).

"If the body is upright—or uptight, so will be the spirit and the mind," I often say. A physical therapist tells me people in wheelchairs often sit more upright than others slouching at their computers. Opening one's physical self releases the psyche, freeing us to discern the rhythms of grace. Pause now, and breathe deeply. Imagine breathing in as receiving the gift of life… then imagine breathing out as giving back… Enjoy the rhythm of receiving… giving… as you pray the following poem.

Poiéma

Your body is a poem
and its tempo
is in your breathing—
in... out...

Your body is a poem
and its meter
is in your walking—
left... right...

Your body is a poem
and its rhythm
is in your hands—
clasping... releasing...

Your body is a poem
and its cadence
is in your turning—
backwards... forwards...

Your body is a poem
and its nodes
are in your brain—
thinking... sensing...

Your body is a poem
and its haiku
is in your eye—
beholding... holding...

Your body is a poem
and its beat
is in your heart—
touch it... feel it...

End by placing your fingers on your pulse (on your wrist, chest, or neck). Imagine aligning your heart with the divine heartbeat at the center of the universe.

How can we honor the body? Cultivate habits of the heart for exercising, walking, breathing, eating, sleeping, meditating, releasing stress, caring for self, and tending to our posture.

"Sweating My Way Home": Tobin's term paper topic held my attention as he reflected on an encounter with God during a cross-cultural trip doing construction work. Sometimes, as in monastic communities, physical work is a spiritual discipline. As I write this, I'm going on another building project with Habitat for Humanity. Always I experience moments of physical exhaustion that seem to pave the way for moments of spiritual exhilaration. In France peasant workers would use an expression if an apprentice got tired or injured, "It is the trade entering his body."

Sometimes we *yearn* our way home—breathing and groaning becomes our inarticulate praying (see Romans 8:18-26). Or we *think* our way home, like C.S. Lewis. Other times, like Tobin, we *sweat* our way home. Body language is our primary speech.

All these may interface—through joy or through pain. We can pray with *breath, brains,* and *brawn.*

The body can bring us home through the joy of life-giving sexuality: we sweat, we groan, we know beyond words. Since 1974, when I injured my back, I have known times of intense pain. I practice a regimen of physical therapy exercises to strengthen the muscles and prevent further pain. I've found ways to incorporate liturgical prayers, scriptures, breathing meditations, imagination and centering prayer with physical exercises.

The body holds the golden key to savoring life's ecstatic moments and for releasing painful stress and converting it into focused spiritual and vocational energy.

SPIRITUAL PRACTICE 4: MEDITATIVE THANKS WITH THE BODY

Sit in stillness, slow down your breathing. Allow a centering word or image to arise. Slowly, using the image or word, inhale lovingly ... meditate ... exhale thankfully .... Begin by *tensing* your left foot (inhaling), then *releasing* (exhaling) ... repeat with the right foot ... the left ankle ... the right ankle, etc., each area of the body up through your abdomen ... to your heart ... then each shoulder ... each arm... each hand ... your larynx ... parts of the face ... to the top of your head ... Enjoy an aura of peace. Imagine this as a kind of "rosary with your body," joining the whole body of Christ.

QUESTIONS FOR PERSONAL OR GROUP REFLECTION

1. What are some ways you "pray" with your body—though you might not have thought of some of them as prayer?
2. What are some ways you care for your body as the "temple" of the Spirit?
3. How does physical work or exercise become prayer for you?
4. How do you celebrate joy with your body? In solitude? In community? In liturgy? In work?
5. Scanning over your life, can you notice times when pain has been transformed into energy and purpose?

5

Busy vs. Active:
Stillness While in Motion

The one who sees the inaction that is in action and the action that is in inaction, is wise indeed. Even when engaged in action, one remains poised in tranquility.

—The Bhagavad Gita

"I know you're really busy, pastor, but ..." That refrain for many of us is like nails on a blackboard. To such a comment, I often reply, "It is an active time, but your concern is important for both of us," and we continue the conversation. But if I know the person well enough, I may say more.

I've tried to delete the word busy from my vocabulary, even in my own self-talk. I can be active and contemplative, I tell myself; the words even rhyme. But being busy and contemplative is a theological oxymoron.

Still while moving. "Busy, busy, busy ..." With such an outer landscape, it's nearly impossible to silence the inner landscape. "Be still, and know that I am God" (Psalm 46:10). You might think of this as "prayer in reverse": it's you listening while God speaks, whispering into the recesses of your heart.

While leading a clergy workshop on "Spiritual Practices for Ministry" in Hershey, Pennsylvania, I suggested going away to the nearby Jesuit Center for an overnight and a day of silent personal retreat. "Take nothing with you but your Bible and a journal, no other books," I said. "Just listen to the books already written on your heart. Don't go to plan your sermons; just listen to the sermons already hidden in your heart."

As I tell this story two decades later, I still recall with pathos a bright young pastor leaning forward and saying, "I would go stir crazy if I had to be silent for even half a day." My sadness was not about his rejecting a silent retreat; it was about the overwhelming sense that he was a stranger to himself.

"All of humanity's problems stem from [one's] inability to sit quietly in a room alone," said Blaise Pascal. When a pastor says, "My people aren't comfortable with silence," translate, "I'm not comfortable with silence." Here is where the inward practices and outward ministry dovetail. One fruit for a pastor who practices being at home in oneself and God in silence is that one more likely allows pauses in conversations to listen to another, and brief pauses in worship, even while preaching or teaching.

"To achieve stillness, that is not difficult. Ah, but to achieve stillness while in motion, that is the miracle," to paraphrase the Dancing Wu Li Master. Thomas Merton concludes in his bestselling *Seven Storey Mountain*: "Saint Thomas [Aquinas] taught that there were three vocations: that to the active life, that to the contemplative, and a third to the mixture of both, and that this last is superior to the other two."[6]

The paradoxical third way. Spiritual practices facilitate this paradoxical active contemplative way.

Intentional prayer. The active contemplative life is a call to design a regular set-aside time for holistic exercises: verbal prayer, centering prayer or body prayer; meditating with scripture, journaling, spiritual reading and the like. But avoid trying for perfection (see Chapter 10).

Prayer throughout the day. Practicing the contemplative active life means integrating prayerful pauses throughout the day. Such a practice release stress, allow for more creativity, restore energy and renew one's spiritual center. To every one who meets with me for spiritual companioning I give a bookmark with these words from Alcoholics Anonymous so-called "Big Book."

> As we go through the day we pause, when agitated or doubtful, and ask for the right thought or action. We constantly remind ourselves we are no longer running

the show, humbly saying to ourselves many times each day "Thy will be done."* We are then in much less danger of excitement, fear, anger, worry, self-pity, or foolish decisions. We become much more efficient. We do not tire so easily for we are not burning up energy foolishly as we did when we were trying to arrange life to suit ourselves."[7] *Or another centering phrase.

Spiritual guidance. To cultivate an active contemplative ministry, clergy and lay leaders find they need the spiritual accountability of meeting monthly with a spiritual guide one-to-one or with colleagues committed to group spiritual guidance (see Resource Two).

Personal retreat. The integrative life of action and contemplation needs the rhythm of one or two solitary retreats a year, with the guidance of a spiritual mentor (either planning and reflecting with one's through-the-year spiritual guide or with a guide at a retreat center).

In *The Violence of Love,* a journalist asked Oscar Romero, the martyred archbishop of San Salvador, what kept him going despite so many threats on his life. Recently returned from another personal retreat, Romero answered that if it were not for prayer and reflection he would be no more than what St. Paul calls "clanging metal."

As I write this, I've just met with a young companion fresh back from making a silent personal retreat. In sharp contrast to the pastor who said he would go stir crazy in silence, this pastor is not a stranger to himself. He bears witness to the rejuvenating power of befriending solitude.

SPIRITUAL PRACTICE 5: YOUR PORTABLE MONASTERY

Here's a method for integrating "monastic" practices in the stress of everyday life. After working for some time on the phone or at the computer or other project, push your chair back a few inches, with your lap and hands empty (or if you're standing, find a corner of the room to rest against.) Take a few deep breaths ... let a line of a poem, scripture, or centering word to come to mind—such as *shalom* (peace) or *amor* (love), or trust. Begin to repeat it slowly, in rhythm to your breathing. You have entered your portable monastery. After a minute or so, pull your chair back to your work area (or reenter the space) ... and resume working. OPTION: Place an icon, a bell or chime at your workspace; push back to meditate on the icon, or the sound of the chime or bell. (A group example: Try this exercise during a committee or group meeting.)

QUESTIONS FOR PERSONAL OR GROUP REFLECTION:

1. What is your experience with cultivating meditative pauses in your working day?
2. What do you see as some of the benefits of a set-aside time for prayer and meditation? What are some of the barriers that get in the way?
3. How could some of the barriers actually become an invitation to go more deeply?

6

Praying on the Go: Practicing *Lectio Divina* in All of Life

If one looks long enough at almost anything, looks with absolute attention at a flower, a stone, the bark of a tree, grass, snow, a cloud, something like revelation takes place …. We are aware of God only when we cease to be aware of ourselves, not in the negative sense of denying the self, but in the sense of losing self in admiration and joy."

—May Sarton

Not all praying happens sitting still. The time-honored Benedictine method for reading and meditating with scripture, *lectio divina* (literally "divine reading"), provides a transferable spiritual practice to sharpen our vision in reading and contemplating all of life.

The scriptural *lectio divina* can be adapted to any text—poetry, fiction, or literature—and to all of life. By expanding the *lectio* process we restore it to its original role of creating spiritual literacy in the rhythms of contemplation and action.[8]

Traditional lectio divina. In the fifth century, Benedict of Nursia used an earthy metaphor of the *lectio* process: Read a short text meditatively—like a cow chewing her cud—until you begin to delight in the presence of God. In the twelfth century, Guigo the Carthusian framed Benedict's *lectio* in four stages: reading (grazing); meditating (chewing); praying (ruminating); contemplating (digesting, resting). The word has now become flesh in the reader.

You read until a short phrase or image in the text begins to lure you, or disturb you, and you follow where it leads. Ignatius of Loyola's method of meditation adds the special use of imagination. In his early romantic life, Ignatius would read fictional love and war stories and visualize the scenes. Abruptly holed up in a Spanish castle after a serious leg injury, he used the same method with the Gospel portraits of Jesus and found himself drawn in to the sights and sounds and characters in the stories. I liken the process to reading a text and then creating your own inner Hollywood set.

Experience before words. Ages before the ancient practice of *lectio* created a process for converting printed words into lived experience; it began as a process of converting experience into living words. First came Moses' vision of the burning bush, or the Buddha's childhood memory of sitting under the Bo tree. Then came the recorded story as a way to recreate the original experience for future generations.

Jesus compared the luminous word that catches our attention (for Jesus' hearers it was oral) to the image of seed: some falls on rocky ground, some on hard ground, some on good soil (see Mark 4:3-20). Cultivating our attentiveness and receptivity creates the good soil. Thomas Merton picks up this metaphor in *New Seeds of Contemplation:*

> Every moment and every event of every person's life on earth plants something in one's soul. For just as the wind carries thousands of winged seeds, so each moment brings with it germs of spiritual vitality that come to rest imperceptibly in the minds and wills of human beings. Most of these unnumbered seeds perish and are lost, because people are not prepared to receive them: for such seeds as these cannot spring up anywhere except in the good soil of freedom, spontaneity and love.[9]

The *lectio* process creates a way to let seeds of love catch you, so that you can live and love purposefully and spontaneously, with discipline and freedom. Theologians from Chrysostom to Augustine onward speak of the book of scripture and the book of nature. This broader application of *lectio* pays serious attention to incarnation—the divine word embodied in our most worldly experiences of nature and human nature.

The luminous particular. Poet Jane Kenyon's vivid metaphor "the luminous particular" aptly describes both directions of the *lectio divina* process: to convert experience into words—written or proclaimed—and to convert words into experience. Kenyon's aim in the lyric poem is to take a striking event or experience and craft it with such telling detail, crisp language, and physical imagery that the reader feels present.[10] Translate this to preaching (see Chapter 14).

Two examples put flesh on the ancient *lectio* method, applying it to "reading" all of life, like the poet Blake seeing "the world in a grain of sand."

Born unable to speak or see, a young woman was determined to communicate. After many struggles, one day her teacher pumped and spelled w-a-t-e-r on her hand. Said Helen Keller, "I understood that what my teacher was doing with her fingers meant that the cold something that was rushing over my hand was water." She wrote, "There was a strange stir within me—a misty consciousness, a sense of something remembered."[11] The mystery of language was revealed to her. One luminous moment opened a new world.

An 11-year-old was watching a news clip showing a homeless man sleeping on the street in downtown Philadelphia on a bitter cold night. Trevor Farrell insisted his parents drive him from their suburban Gladwyne home to the city that night. Ignoring his mother's plea merely to open the car window, he darted from the car to hand the man his own blanket and pillow. A single TV news clip had spread its roots in Trevor, until eventually his father quit his job and the family formed a non-profit organization, Trevor's Place.[12]

Delight or disturb. The two stories show how a *lectio* moment may delight (as with Keller) or disturb (as with Farrell). Life is filled with luminous particulars that want to arrest our attention to crack open the seed of our souls. Genuine insights come wrapped in awe. But awe can appear to us as awesome or awful—or a paradoxical interplay of both.

The secret for staying awake to the sacred lines in all of life is the practice of recollection, harvesting *and* reflecting on "luminous particulars" along the journey.

SPIRITUAL PRACTICE 6: PRACTICING *LECTIO* IN READING LIFE

Have a page in your journal or paper and pen—or blank computer page ready; put it aside. Scan over a recent period of your life: conversations, chance encounters, books you've read, movies you've seen, places you've visited, dreams you've had. Notice any time when a line of a conversation or a movie scene, a dream fragment or an experience of nature, arrested your attention—*delighted* or *disturbed* you. Sit for few more minutes in silence, simply being with that experience. Now, begin to write, recalling as many here-and-now particulars as possible. At some point put down your pen or pencil—or pull back from the keypad. Read over what you've written and notice "luminous particular" phrases, metaphors, or images. Underline or highlight them. Read it to someone, or ask a person read it back to you. Reflect a second time on poignant phrases and images; then meditate with one of them. Do you sense any new insight or word for your life?

QUESTIONS FOR PERSONAL OR GROUP REFLECTION:

1. Engage in the exercise above. In recalling such a lived moment, what new layers of awareness, meaning or hope speaks to you now?
2. In what ways does reflecting on such a lived moment draw you more deeply into your own self and soul? Does it connect you more closely with others?

7

Clergy Table Talk: God Outside Our Religious Boxes

I have discovered that I am deeply interested in the way "God talk" enters "street work."

—Arlene Helderman

An out-of-state pastor friend and I were catching up during our annual lunch, when two other pastors and their spouses sat down at a nearby table. Through the din of restaurant noise, we became aware of the echoes of their conversation. It never seemed to veer from church topics—stewardship, worship styles and attendance, new members, conflict with denominational leadership. For about an hour they engaged in churchy shoptalk.

Later, my friend and I commented how common it is for us clergy to drift into church talk when we get together. I recalled a prophetic moment from my Penn State days, while attending an InterVarsity Christian Fellowship leadership retreat at Cedar Campus on Michigan's Upper Peninsula. One evening's speaker said something like, "This afternoon I noticed several of you talking about spiritual things while seemingly oblivious to nature's beauty all about you—the crystalline lake, the cobalt sky, butternut saplings, ancient tamaracks, gigantic birch, amazing flora and fauna." I took away a message that if you want to relate Christ to people you need to relate to the world around you.

Practicing the craft of inter-being. From the world of finance I learned "interest follows investment." This is a so true in relationships: when I ask someone a simple question I am investing a bit of my self. "Interest" (Latin *interesse*) means "inter-being." What if we just began taking more interest in each other?

People literally die of loneliness. How can we delve more deeply within our souls, even in brief encounters? How can we cultivate among clergy the kind of atmosphere that if a non-religious person were to appear, they might feel drawn to the conversation?

From serious to playful. I recall a mentor saying that in spiritual direction, when a person talks mostly about God or serious stuff, we need to ask things like: What are you doing for play? What movies have you seen lately? What sorts of things are you reading?

I confess sometimes I freeze when someone asks me such questions, yet I always appreciate the challenge. Twenty minutes later I'll think, "Oh, why didn't I mention reading Kathryn Stockett's *The Help* or how late at night I got drawn into rereading Pablo Neruda's poetry?" I sometimes use my "forget" as a chance to go back to the person to say thanks for their inquiry, then to tell my recalled insights. It comes as affirmation to return to a person and deepen a conversation.

My movie memory used to seem like a sieve, so some years ago I began a ritual of writing each movie title with key actors and theme, and the date I saw it, in a section in the back of my journal. It's served me well, because as I prepare to preach or write, I can scan over the titles and think: *Ah, here's a story that will flesh out this idea!* And somehow, the mere act of writing down each movie seems to aid my on-the-spot conversations.

Feeling dislocated. After two decades as a pastor of congregations, when I left the parish to engage in specialized ministries of chaplaincy and spiritual formation, I experienced first-hand a subtle dislocation during conversations many ministers unwittingly engage in. I checked out my perceptions with parish pastors who are African American, Korean, Hispanic and women. They said basically, "We feel out of the loop most of the time when we're with normal agenda-driven pastors."

Asking thoughtful questions helps break the shoptalk impasse (see Chapter 8). When meeting a new clergyperson, pretty soon after a few exchanges about places we've lived, schools we've attended, and ministry contexts where we've served, I may ask: What are some things you like to do for play? Or, how do you spend some of your time when not working? If she or he is new in town, what are some of your desires for your new ministry? Always one hopes to evoke a reciprocal conversation, and often it happens.

Mini lab experiments. We can delve more deeply with colleagues we already know by asking, what's something going on that you find energizing in your life—or in your ministry? It's drawing on the Appreciative Inquiry style of connecting with a person's strengths, yet it seems to avoid the one-upmanship trap. If you're attentive, even without asking directly, you'll often hear hints of tension and stress silhouetting the joys. You know then you have dropped into really fertile turf. These are the kinds of segues that can lead to an invitation to find (or found) a clergy colleague group or to engage in spiritual companioning, one-to-one, or in a group setting.

Subliminally, a kind of informal *lectio divna* can begin to happen in our relationships and in ministry: gently recalling a line of a conversation or a scene in a movie or an experience of nature that arrests your attention—that delights or disturbs you (see Chapter 6). Authentic clergy gatherings can begin to function as mini laboratory experiments to permeate the walls of our religious boxes and relate to people who yearn for meaningful human and spiritual connections. Many, like Arlene Helderman, are interested in how "God talk" enters "street work." So our clergy table talk can leaven our table talk with hungry folks outside the doors of our worship houses.

SPIRITUAL PRACTICE 7: LAB EXPERIMENTS WITH CLERGY GATHERINGS

The next time you find yourself in a clergy group, a carpool or a denominational meeting, pray that it can become a lab experiment for dropping into deeper conversations and relationships. Try out fresh questions of your own, or some of the ones above. How do you spend some of your time when not working? What's something going on that you find energizing in your life—or your ministry? What do you do for play? What movies have you seen lately? What sorts of things have you been reading? Be prayerfully aware of how the Spirit may be speaking a new word to you through your colleagues' responses.

QUESTIONS FOR PERSONAL OR GROUP REFLECTION:

1. Reflect on the questions above and any "lab experiment" with a clergy group. What was it like to try out different ways of relating?
2. Did the process feel a bit edgy? If so, how did that draw you to prayerfulness?
3. Did you experience any shift while conversing? Any moment of awkwardness? Any surprise twist in relating to another clergy colleague?

8
Spiritual Direction: The Yin and Yang of Questions and Stories

If I had an hour to solve a problem and my life depended on the solution, I would spend the first 55 minutes determining the proper question to ask, for once I know the proper question, I could solve the problem in less than five minutes.

—Albert Einstein

There are so many stories, more beautiful than answers.

—Mary Oliver

Waiting for a stoplight at a five-point intersection near Hershey, Pennsylvania, I thought, "I could turn right and go see Sister Marion (my spiritual director then) about a troubling situation. But by the time the light turned green, I knew the question she would ask me. I drove straight home.

I knew the question she would ask: not what she would tell me—not advice or answers. For me, that moment offers a paradigm for spiritual companioning: the direction begins to happen within the soul of the seeker. Such guidance opens up rather than closes down one's spirit.

In my twenties I was listening to a mentor give an after-dinner talk on communication. Just as an aside he said, "And as we all know, insight is not transferable." As we *all* know?—I queried to myself. The line never let go of me.

Thoughtful questions. Somewhere along life's way, it occurred to me when I feel an insight coming on, to hold it back and fast from it a bit, to see if I can convert my insight into a *question*.

This creates three spiritual movements. First, to convert an insight into a question creates a pause while this mini-conversion takes place my own psyche. Second, I momentarily lose control. By my talking, I keep another passive; I can give advice. Asking creates a pause, makes me vulnerable: where is this going to go? Third, the other person also has to pause and ponder the question—slowing down the rapid-fire train of thought.

Turning an insight into a question works wonders in parenting, human relations, management, teaching, preaching, and life. You cannot teach the art of contemplation, yet an ordinary query can induce what the philosopher Lessing called "the creative pause." Such a pregnant moment allows for a mini-*kenosis*, a bit of empty space like rests in a musical score—where whatever we mean by insight or wonder or grace can creep in. And wonder working is what mystery is all about.

A young person insisted on wanting a doctoral program, yet seemed hesitant. I was tempted to suggest she was afraid of failure. Instead, I asked: What's your deepest fear? She began with fears about money, time—maybe failing. She paused. This whole grad school idea was really based on a fear of not measuring up to her older brother. "I need to pursue *my own* vision," she said. Had I told my insight, she might have missed her own.

Learning to convert little ideas in conversations into questions can train us to welcome life's big questions—to live into the answer some future day. In *Big Questions, Worthy Dreams,* Sharon Daloz Parks asserts that many young adults are being cheated:

> "*They are not being asked big-enough questions.* They are not being invited to entertain the greatest questions of their own lives and of their times .... What do I really want to become? When do I feel most alive? Where can I be creative? What am I vulnerable to? What are my fears? ... Why is there a growing gap between the haves and the have-nots? Why is the prison population growing in the United States? Why

are antidepressants being prescribed for increasing numbers of children? What are the reasons for climate change?[13]

Questions open up insights from within and afar. Is this not what spiritual leadership is all about—coaching others to open to unknown Wisdom?

Powerful stories. Frequently a thoughtful question spawns a story, and that is the second way that insight may emerge without giving direct advice. "There are so many stories, more beautiful than answers," wrote Mary Oliver.[14]

Every time I "die" to one of my own insights and watch it rise creatively in another I witness a mini-resurrection. Like questions, a well-chosen story creates a momentary suspension of preconceived ideas.

Research shows that technical information stimulates the *left* sphere of the brain (the place of linguistic, logical, and linear thinking). And the *right* sphere (the place rhythmic, artistic, creative thinking) is stimulated by music, art, and dance. But when *stories* are fed to the brain, something amazing happens: both spheres are stimulated.

The multiple intelligences approach of Howard Gardner provides a lens to awaken the soul's "true self" in all arenas of life. Stories utilize all nine learning modes for mending the interrupted narratives of our lives (see Chapter 3).

Stories are vehicles for transmitting life: They contain a "story line" employing *language*—using linear thinking and *logic*. Stories create *space* through imagination, and often contain *music*—or they are made into musicals or ballads. Stories are *kinesthetic*, embodied in gestures, drama and dance. Stories create *intrapersonal* movements in the heart and *interpersonal* relationships among hearers. Stories contain *naturalist* images—the mystery of devastation and renewal, violence and beauty. *Existentialist* intelligence asks, How can we find meaning in all the rhythms of life?

Questions and stories form the yin and the yang of learning to yearn for one's deepest desires—as in the methods of Krishna, the

Buddha, Lao Tzu, Socrates, Hillel or Jesus. A good question or a good story is more life giving than any ready-made answer.

In her masterpiece *Their Eyes Were Watching God,* Zora Neale Hurston writes: "There are years that ask questions and years that answer."[15] The treasures of our stories often remain locked like unclaimed baggage in the dark corners of unexamined years that long to answer.

Struggles with stories and questions. As clergy, people often want answers from us. Too often we take the bait, needing to sound wise, avoiding the risk of deeper conversation, even conversion. Yet a discerning question or story can save us from simplistic answers and help us understand what's going on in the person, so our answer doesn't go wide of the mark.

We struggle with another issue. "Is it OK for a preacher to tell personal stories?" someone asked John Killinger in a Q&A session. "Yes," the renowned preacher pondered, "it's all right to share personal stories—as long as it puts the preacher in the position of being a recipient of grace." No one believes a triumphalist pastor. Henri Nouwen's writings still speak so profoundly because he shared his own brokenness on the road to wholeness.

The downside of stories. Without the art of story listening, storytelling can be demeaning. In *The Art of Racing in the Rain,* Garth Stein's dog Enzo tells us why he would be a good person in a future life: "Because I listen. I cannot speak, so I listen very well. I never interrupt; I never deflect the course of the conversation with a comment of my own. People, if you pay attention to them, change the direction of one another's conversations constantly. It's like having a passenger in your car who suddenly grabs the steering wheel and turns you down a side street." Says Enzo: "I beg you. Pretend you are a dog like me and listen to other people rather than steal their stories."[16]

All of us have been with a person, who, upon hearing the story of your mother's cancer, instead of showing an interest and asking you a question, immediately grabs the steering wheel and drives you to the scene of their own mother's funeral.

The downside of questions. After being injured in a head-on car crash, my wife was hospitalized for 38 days. Many of my clergy colleagues came to visit. Most made brief calls and she felt understood and cared for. But she grew to dread seeing one minister. "His probing questions wear me out," she said. "Why do they have you on that intravenous tube? How long till you can eat solid food? When will they reverse your colostomy?" Learning the art of asking thoughtful and powerful questions can transform relationships, committees, teaching and preaching. See "The Art of Powerful Questions": http://LinkYourSpirituality.com/ articles.html

Finding spiritual direction. As clergy we serve as de facto spiritual guides for others, in the parking lot or the study, in sermons and committee meetings, at deathbeds and weddings, with church folks and our own families. So it behooves each of us to have a trusted spiritual companion (director, mentor, guide) or group. This can serve as a laboratory to practice the art of discernment through another's listening to our own stories and asking us meaningful questions. For a spiritual guide near you, see Spiritual Directors International: www.sdiworld.org and click on seek and find.

SPIRITUAL PRACTICE 8. ASKING QUESTIONS, TELLING STORIES

Seize occasions to experiment in the coming week. Try making an observation and/or asking a question instead of giving an insight: "I noticed a metaphor you used (repeating what the person said); I wonder, what is that about?" Or, if a story comes to mind more than once while conversing, you might share it. Gently ask if there might be any connection for the other person. Allow pauses to draw you deeper into trusting love in the Ground of your being.

FOR PERSONAL OR GROUP REFLECTION

1. Describe an occasion in recent weeks when you have served as an intentional or a *de facto* spiritual guide for someone. What were the circumstances? What were the qualities of the conversation? What was the ratio of speaking, listening and questions?

2. Turn it around. Describe an occasion in recent weeks when someone else served as an intentional or a *de facto* spiritual guide for you. What were the circumstances? What were the qualities of the conversation? What was the ratio of speaking, listening and questions?

3. What sense of invitation do you take away from this chapter?

9

Negative Capability:
Prozac Days and Dark Nights

An unanswered question is a fine traveling companion.
It sharpens your eye for the road.

—Rachael Naomi Remen

The opposite of depression is not happiness but vitality,
and my life, as I write this is vital, even when sad.

—Andrew Solomon

I was hosting the local minister's group at the church I was newly serving, when the longest-term pastor showed up early. Over coffee, I began speaking about a few of my struggles. He said, "I've never been depressed a day in my life." (I was glad another minister arrived.) Though I had never said I was depressed, I had lost a potential mentor. I felt sad for him and for his congregation, because no person or parson escapes depression's shadow, directly or indirectly.

Ambiguous blessings. The unspoken taboo against emotional (in contrast to physical) illness in religious communities leaves masses of spiritual folks painfully orphaned: "If you had faith you'd be happy." The diagnosis of bipolar disorder, manic depression's new name, is exponentially on the rise among younger generations.[17] Imaginative people have always known depression's ambiguous blessings. Our tragic romantic personalities help us dream the impossible but also catapult us into dark holes.

Medication can keep a person from going over the edge, as I myself can testify. But ah, would that depression's cure were so simple as a new pill. What about the social matrix contributing to this runaway cultural plague? Meanwhile huge numbers of children swell the ranks of adults who struggle with this crazy mystery. The concept of emptiness offers a unique spiritual perspective on this increasing social pain of depression, while offering room for medical forms of treatment.

Negative capability. In a letter to his brother dated December 21, 1817, poet John Keats gave us a profound phrase that's found its way into science, literature and spirituality. He tells how he was walking home from a Christmas pageant with two friends. Keats describes one of them, Dilke, as a person who has "already made up his mind about everything": he would never learn anything new. In a moment of irritation, Keats's insight dropped in.

> Several things dovetailed in my mind, and at once it struck me what quality went to form a Man of Achievement, especially in Literature & which Shakespeare possessed so enormously—I mean *Negative Capability*, that is, when man is capable of being in uncertainties, Mysteries, doubts, without an irritable reaching after fact & reason.[18]

Our culture programs us to value answers and productivity. Yet every creative person knows that empty space (the Greeks called it *kenosis*), the void of unknowing, is the womb for a new creation, as in the primal creation: "And the earth was a formless void and darkness was on the face of the deep" (Genesis 1:3).

Novelists speak of emptying their own personality in order to enter the characters they write about. Werner Heisenberg, Nobel Prize winner for his famous Uncertainty Principle of quantum physics, would speak to his researcher in the middle of some problem. "Wait, I think we have touched something very important here. Let's not talk about it ... Let's wait for two weeks, and let it solve itself."[19] John Woolman, who walked on foot to urge Quakers to free their slaves in the 1700s, tells in his *Journals* how often his act of saying nothing in a Friends' Meeting had more impact than words.

Emptiness in spiritual traditions. The New Testament urges disciples to practice the mindset of Christ Jesus who "emptied" himself (*kenosis* in Greek) to the point of death—even though equal to God according to Paul (Philippians 2:5-11).

The Buddhist experience of *Sunyata* as emptiness, and *zimzum* as divine self-emptying in the Jewish Kabala, draw Christians back to our own truth: the self-emptying *kenosis* of Christ is not just an event in history or a belief in one's head, but is a "mindset" to be practiced, a day-by-day experience of *kenosis* in one's personal history.

This inner mindset of emptiness is counter-cultural. It sounds very Eastern yet it marks the character of every disciple. For Christians, *kenosis* means living out one's baptism, dying and rising in Christ. It means letting go of one's own preconceived ideas—whether of self-inflation or self-deprecation—then opening oneself to surprise possibilities.

Emptying oneself into a cause. Sometimes you experience *kenosis* by immersing yourself in passionate action. You empty yourself of any attachments to consequences; you are free to act with love.

In *The Shawshank Redemption,* a movie based on Stephen King's novel, Andy Dufresne (Tim Robbins) is wrongly convicted of shooting his cheating wife and her lover. As prison librarian, he receives LP records. Locking the warden in the bathroom, Andy boldly enters the prison office and plays a Mozart duet over the sound system. Prisoners inside rise from sleep; outside they stand at attention. Red (Morgan Freeman) describes the music as "so beautiful it can't be expressed in words, and makes your heart ache because of it.... It was like some beautiful bird flapped into our drab little cage and made these walls dissolve away... and for the briefest of moments—every last man at Shawshank felt free." Then Freeman's voice announces that Andy "got two weeks in the hole for that stunt."[20]

Genuine humility means following your passion to bless people—like Gandhi, King, or Rosa Parks. Love frees you to claim your gifts and risk being thrown into a dark hole.

Dark Night of the Soul and Depression. I'm learning to befriend silence and emptiness to free myself from attachments and open myself for courage and creativity. But "blessed are the poor in spirit" is never an easy blessing whether by choice or circumstance. For me, writing into the tides of my own bipolar disorder is one such difficult blessing.

The dark night of the soul is not to be equated with psychological depression. Depression's sources vary from an innate chemical imbalance to outward life crises like abuse, death, divorce, or acute disappointment in oneself or others. Therapy can help; so can medications, like a cast for a broken bone or like insulin for diabetes. But I believe a spiritual lens on this ambivalent blessing is not a luxury but essential to staying vital even when sad.

A student asked her therapist, what would be the difference between depression and dark night? The counselor paused—then said, "The outcome." One person may enter a crisis with no recovery. A second may go through a vocational or marriage crisis, then find a new job or a new relationship and recover functionally, yet with no apparent spiritual transformation. A third may go through the same outward crisis and undergo a spiritual transformation hidden in the night of crisis.

For yet another, the transforming night arrives unbidden and unrelated to any biochemical imbalance or outward crisis: "Even the darkness is not dark to you; the night is bright as the day, for darkness is as light to you" (Psalm 139:12). For each, the promise is the same, as God speaks through Isaiah: "I will give you treasures of darkness, riches hidden in secret places" (45:3).

That treasure is love, even when I despair for want of feeling it. "Depression is the flaw in love, writes Andrew Solomon in *The Noonday Demon: An Atlas of Depression*. "To be creatures who love, we must be creatures who can despair at what we lose, and depression is the mechanism of that despair."²¹ Those demons have visited me.

Night Demons

They come in the night,
these demons of self-doubt—
they come to disqualify me,
kidnapping my confidence:
How can you be spiritual
yet be this anxious?
How dare you offer
your needy self to be
a spiritual guide for others?

Then the Spirit comes—
to comfort, to console,
fortifying me with
the ancient assurance
that I am one beggar
showing other beggars
where to find bread,
that my very neediness
validates my credentials,
as one who surely seeks
and just as surely finds,
—as one already found.

I've gone through the yoyo of emptiness and gestation while writing *Clergy Table Talk*. Stuck times create a pause to ponder, like *Selah* in the Psalms. Writing now about pausing calls me to pause again... After some silence, I write in my journal: *Who am I to write this book with so much restlessness?* I write into the restlessness, the ferment ... Then I conclude: *With so much restlessness, who am I not to write this book?* I return again as a child: *Befriending what is changes what was—and what will be.*

I call this the "theology of the fishhook." You write down deep into the stuck place ... then you find a mini-upswing that catches a new insight. When you're stuck with the sermon, write about what you can't write about. Then you're no longer stuck.

Depression and anger. I can never forget Mary's "teaching" in the wake of riots and assassinations in the late 1960s. Recruited from the streets of Westside Chicago to educate us minister-types for urban ministry, Mary would say, "Apathy is frozen rage." Like a liturgical refrain during this month-long program when anyone recounted a surprise incident of violence, we would hear it again: "Like I say, apathy's just frozen rage."

That Fall I took a course on "The Psychology of Education" at the University of Chicago from Allison Davis, author of a classic series on descendants of slaves, *The Eighth Generation*. (I recall my delight two decades later when he was featured on an African American heritage postage stamp.) The class could be summed up in Davis's repeated phrase: "Depression is anger turned inward." It sounded only a tad more scholarly and Freudian than Mary's refrain; I was sure the two had colluded.

Transformation. Befriending emptiness calls me back to attention, like a child. I notice two things: First, often I find anger beneath the depression, and anger is energy. Apathy's spell is broken; I can see depression as negative capability.

Second, I feel depressed because I feel out of sync with the world, like most creative people—like many clergy as you read this. Seeing oneself as a misfit can release energy for good: witness Jesus and a host of misfits in his train—from Saint Paul to Saint Francis, Van Gogh to Mozart, Martin Luther King, Jr. to Mother Teresa. Out-of-the box pioneers validate other lonely pilgrims. Negative capability.

Ultimately the conversion process of seeing so-called negative emotions as capability is not something we do at all, but a transformation worked in us. Spiritual practices like silence, writing, and the arts befriend the soul's desire for transformation.

In the film *The Matrix*, Thomas is transformed when he begins to doubt the dehumanizing matrix surrounding his work. His anger at the system then causes him to listen to the (phone) call to freedom. We are blessed when we begin to discover the gift of negative capability in times of doubt, confusion, and anger, moving us to contemplate a new sense of call.

A spiritual lens. Like diabetes, if mental illness requires medical treatment use it. Or like a broken leg, use crutches till it heals. But unlike physical illness, because of the shame our culture projects on us who suffer emotional pain, I believe a spiritual lens on this goofy gory gift is not a luxury, but essential to staying vital—even when you feel sad or when others think you are wacko.

If you (or one of your flock) are on crutches or insulin or Prozac, one can still meet with a spiritual companion (yes, perhaps you), to talk about patterns of meaning in one's spiritual journey and where it's leading. That can color prosaic days with nighttime's mysterious intimacy.

SPIRITUAL PRACTICE 9: EMPTINESS AS SPACE FOR LOVE

Be still and attentive to some emptiness in your life: an unfulfilled desire you may rarely express. Gently get in touch with it. One somewhat private person said, "It was that my mother died and never got to see my husband and children." It may be a kind of a spiritual homing instinct, "a God-shaped vacuum." Gently look at ways you may be using to fill it, or deny it—creative, or destructive. Prayerfully, offer the emptiness by framing it as "space for Love."[22] What are some ways you can befriend the emptiness, for example, by sculpting it, dancing it, painting it, preaching or writing into it, making a poem or music of it? What would it look like just to allow the emptiness to be?

QUESTIONS FOR PERSONAL OR GROUP REFLECTION

1. Everyone deals with disappointment and emptiness, often with mild or major periods of depression. What are some transformative responses you have found helpful in such times—medical, psychological, vocational, recreational or physical?
2. In what sense have some of your responses to such periods become for you glimpses into a kind of dark night of the soul?
3. What are some inward and outward fruits of such soul struggles?

10

Grace in the Grit:
Exorcising the Demon of
Perfectionism

Once in a while you can get shown the light
in the strangest of places if you look at it right.
—Robert Hunter

While writing this, I found grace in the grit of working on an adobe-style house for Habitat for Humanity in Taos, New Mexico. Part of me knew I needed spend this precious week writing, but another part knew that the break of engaging in kinesthetic service would be good for my soul and for the writing. The service project won out, and I found myself still "writing" while pounding nails.

Because as volunteer carpenters go and come, each leaving our less-than-perfect doorjambs and windowsills, it creates a funny sort of therapy. A perfectionist would walk off the job at 9a.m. I've come to realize that it's worth several visits to a psychiatrist to cure my perfectionism. Constructing genuine community means building on each other's less than perfect beginnings. My psyche gets healed a bit more when I surround myself with vulnerable human beings on behalf of a good cause.

Never obligation, only invitation. People in western cultures tend to operate out of an all-or-nothing mindset. Go on a diet. Start an exercise routine. Commit to spiritual practices. A year later: It didn't work. I once complained to my orthopedic doctor that the back exercises he prescribed did more harm than good. "I do them for a week; then my back is sorer and I have to quit for two weeks."

"Two things," he said. "First, be gentle on yourself. Exercise till you stretch yourself, but not till you feel intense pain. Second, aim for four days out of seven. If you slip back to three days, just move your inner computer cursor in the right direction." What he told me for my back I give as sound counsel for any physical, mental and spiritual disciplines. I use a phrase: *Never obligation, only invitation.*

Not "Be perfect," rather "Be complete." Religious language reinforces this do-it-right or don't-do-it-at-all attitude. Most folks today mentally translate perfection as perfection*ism,* and perfect as *faultless.* As leaders, we can help people and ourselves with a reminder that both the original New Testament Greek *telios,* and the Latin *perfectum* (behind our English word), mean "complete, mature, or whole." And the Greek noun *telos* means "goal or finish line." One way I script my own psyche is to say, "That's just ideal!—instead of perfect. Our self-talk affects our unconscious thinking and acting.

Jesus does not say, "Be perfect ..." but rather, "Become complete, therefore, as your Abba in heaven is complete" (Matthew 5:48, AT). Luke has already helped by translating the phrase, "Be compassionate* as your Abba is compassionate" (6:36, AT)—and be compassionate to your self. *Or merciful

Our culture inflicts this damning perfectionism on us. A family with a member in recovery from anorexia can witness to the subtle, crippling effects of a Barbie Doll perfection syndrome and exercise addiction. Gerald May, M.D., in *Addiction and Grace,* gives solid counsel for finding inner freedom from all sorts of perfectionist demons. The apostle Paul can say, "Not that I have already obtained this or have already reached the goal (*telos*); but I press on to make it my own, because Christ Jesus has made me his own... Let those of us then who are mature (*telioi*) be of the same mind" (Philippians 3:12, 15).

When I can't take my normal walk in the mornings, I take a mini-walk to keep the pattern going. When I can't take 20 minutes for centering prayer, I take two minutes.

Sabbath. Practicing Sabbath, and pausing for mini-sabbaths, can be an Rx for perfectionism. It's a way of trusting the universe of divine Love to provide for what needs to be done on other days or by other ways or through other folks. To fast from our workaholic tendencies by celebrating with family or friends or self is to claim our humanity and free ourselves from the demon of "it's all about me."

Praying your procrastinations. I'm learning with Ignatius to turn to God in all things—even in my imperfections and procrastinations. I look at envelopes from charitable agencies piling up on my desk; I glance at daily to-do lists, persons to call, to write, to e-mail; I experience human feelings of frustration.

But with some releasing litany—often for me it's a wordless inhaled breath (or a centering word or phrase) followed by a deeply exhaled breath—you can inwardly offer the procrastinations as they come to mind, one by one, while driving or lunching or going to sleep, when it's too late to phone the board chair or make the pastoral visit. Each breath serves as a positive arrow of compassion, instead of a negative downer of guilt.

Through many such yearnings you've prayed countless times for urgent tasks that demanded to be done along the way. Finally, when you do make the phone call, send the e-mail, or write the check, you've wrapped the action in a web of prayers. With a slight inner shift of the sail, you are "turning to God in all things"—praying your procrastinations.

Traces of grace in the grit: Holy humus! A woman on retreat was praying when she heard a construction worker say, "Holy shit!" Later she and I queried: Can this pop phrase mask our human yearning for life's "waste" to morph into wholeness and holiness?

We can take a cue from the visceral spirituality in *The Table Talk of Martin Luther*. Maybe some folks are "praying" without knowing it—that life's lowest places might be consecrated: "Holy humus!" The expression can mean more than venting your spleen. We can pray to see traces of grace in the grit of our own or others' defeats and discouragements.

Grit Seasoning

While I do this grit
work, season
the irksome pieces
with enough
Ahas! to remind me
of the reason.

The reason is your life mission (see Resource Three). It's your "why to live," your purpose for being on this earth, your passion. Such ahas! come unbidden, often just when we feel our own brokenness, even shame and unworthiness.

In a hospital CPE (Clinical Pastoral Education) training program, a new student chaplain was assigned to visit Marie Smith, a patient with terminal cancer; she had called to request a visit. It was this seminarian's first real encounter with death. As he made his way down the hallway in the oncology unit, he was overwhelmed with the stench of necrotic flesh. Upon knocking and then entering the room, he felt overwhelmed by her ashen color. He thought he would throw up. But from somewhere in the back brain, he remembered that it can help at such times to sit down and put your head in your hands. So he sat that way for four or five minutes, and the sickness did lessen.

But when he looked at the woman, he felt so embarrassed by what had happened that he got up and left. Feeling he had failed, he went to the meditation room to sort things out. He decided he would tell his supervisor the next day that he was resigning from the program, and maybe even quitting seminary. Perhaps this ministry thing was not for him.

But the next morning, before he could find the supervisor, she found him. Marie had just called again: Was he the chaplain who visited her? He thought, *Oh no.* "Well, this time she just wanted to say thanks. After she called yesterday, she wished she hadn't; she was so sick she didn't feel like talking, and surely didn't want any minister preaching to her. 'But somehow,' the patient said, 'the chaplain who came must have sensed that. Because he just came in, sat down, bowed his head and prayed for me for maybe five minutes. And then he gave me the most loving glance, and left. Of all my times at this hospital, this is the most meaningful visit I ever received.'"

Once when I told this story, someone asked, "But the chaplain wasn't really praying, was he?" His intense identity with her pain was his visceral praying, his yearning for her with "bowels and mercies" (*splagchna* in Greek; see Philippians 2:1, KJV).

***Felix culpa*: "a good mistake."** Sometimes you can reflect on a story like the chaplain's experience—or a failed project in your congregation or a dumb little thing you did last week—in light of St. Augustine's concept of *felix culpa*. Often it's translated, "happy fault or fortunate fault," referring to the fault/fall of Adam and Eve, which becomes the occasion for each of us to realize the "grace in the grit" as we leave the garden of our own less than perfect lives. I like to translate it: "a good mistake."

Only retroactively do we see good coming out of a failed experiment. But even to frame failure as an "experiment" begins to redeem it. Thomas Edison could say he didn't fail, but found 2,000 ways how not to make the light bulb. Proactively, what we can do is pray to notice flecks of grace in the gaff or the goof—that it can become a good mistake.

"Drops of experience" are never wasted, according to mathematician philosopher Alfred North Whitehead. When you lose computer data on new members, or you drive two hours to a hospital to visit a cancer patient who was just discharged, or you eke away hours learning new technology for a website, tell yourself: *All that time I spent I was praying for new members, or for folks with cancer, or for our congregation to connect with tech generations.*

Here's a really good mistake. In September 1928 Alexander Fleming returned to the laboratory of St. Mary's Hospital in London after being on holiday for a couple of weeks. He discovered Petri dishes that his students mistakenly left in an incubator had formed mold in the dank atmosphere. Fleming noticed—and *noticing* is the miracle of any genuine discovery—that the mold had killed a ring of bacteria. Fleming's surprise discovery of penicillin is a real life story of how a good mistake created the gift of healing for generations. His vacation led to his vocation.

Micromanaging. The need to control people and situations is one of the demonic expressions of perfectionism. At the root of the demon of micromanaging lies a secret fear of shame: I don't want another's half-botched job to reflect poorly on my own self-competence. Another demon behind micromanaging is failing to trust in God by not trusting people.

Humility in a strange way is actually spiritual self-confidence: confidence that you can celebrate the gifts of others, rather than belittle them, while at the same time claiming your own. It's a God-confidence that there are enough gifts for both your neighbor and you to claim your potential for the good of the cosmos, without exploiting or belittling each other. And that's a good definition of *telios:* mature.

SPIRITUAL PRACTICE 10. "LET IT BE"

Listen to the Beatles' song "Let It Be" (on mp3 or the CD *Let It Be*). "Mother Mary" refers to Paul McCartney's dream of his mother, who died when he was fourteen. The title also can be heard as a subtle take on Mary's response when the angel Gabriel announced she would bear a child—seemingly impossible: "Here am I … Let it be to me according to your word" (Luke 1:38). As you hear "Let it be …" in your mind imagine letting go of an issue that you can't control, or accepting a challenge that may want to "birth" itself in you.

(Capital Records, Inc., U.S.A.; Sound recording by EMI Records Ltd., England, 1970)

FOR PERSONAL REFLECTION OR GROUP CONVERSATION

1. How might a shift in language from being "perfect" to being "mature, complete or whole" affect your attitudes and actions? Or affect your expectations of others?
2. How do you see the connection between perfectionism and micromanaging?
3. Humility in a strange way is actually spiritual self-confidence: confidence that you can celebrate and delight in the gifts of others while at the same time claiming your own. How does this strike you?

11
Surprise! Surprise.
Serendipity and Shock in
Ministry

We have two or three great moving experiences in our lives — experiences so great and so moving that it doesn't seem at the time anyone else has been so caught up and pounded and dazzled and astonished and beaten and broken and rescued and illuminated and rewarded and humbled in just that way ever before.

—F. Scott Fitzgerald

Shortly after moving to Denver, I e-mailed Mark, a pastor in his 30s, to reconnect. I was shocked when he wrote back that he was now paralyzed and in wheelchair for life. In the process of removing a benign tumor from his spine, a surgical accident occurred that severed his spinal cord.

For Pastor Liz and Terry, her African American husband and professional musician, racial ostracism reared its head in her congregation upon their arrival in a small US northeastern city. In only months, the irrational rancor ended her ministry there.

"That kind of surprise I don't need," runs an old line. Surprises in ministry and in life can indeed be good medicine for our control needs. However, medicine of this sort is hardly on anyone's clergy wish list.

Surprise can take the form of energizing serendipity like Fleming's discovery of penicillin or a paralyzing shock like 9/11: surprise! or surprise. I aim to show how either kind of surprise—the thrill or the trauma—can be an occasion that leads us to living dead or living awake. What makes the difference?

Responding instead of reacting. Earlier I offered this definition: Spirituality is learning to respond rather than react to events of the world and circumstances of one's life, in a manner that blesses the world and one's own soul. Spiritual practices nurture your learned response in moment of irritation or disaster. Returning to Mark and Liz's ongoing stories, we can see how spiritual practices made a difference in how each responded.

Mark, after discerning that he needed to leave his parish, found a new ministry as a college teacher and campus pastor, while he also gives pastoral leadership to a tiny parish. He's now writing his story as a witness to transforming connections of ministering through disabilities, even while holding open the potential of growing beyond one's limitations.

Liz, thanks to her bright mind and persevering spirit and the flexibility of her musician husband, was able to renegotiate with new denominational leaders. She put together a part-time teaching career with ministering to three small, rural congregations. The small churches loved Terry and utilized his musical gifts. His music has now taken them to New York City where she serves as a church consultant for creative conflict and safe sanctuary training and continues teaching and storytelling workshops.

Each pastor continued meeting with a spiritual guide and engaging in practices of examen, scripture meditation and journaling. Of course it's not that spiritual practices "save" us; it's more like wiping a smudge off the dirtied glass so we can see what's really there. "Prayer means turning to Reality," says Evelyn Underhill in her little classic *The Spiritual Life.*[23] Destructive conflict skews reality; creative conflict sees a deeper Reality.

Lighting fires or putting out fires? Recently I heard from a clergy colleague who served the Episcopal Church in the same small town where I served the Presbyterian Church, in our late twenties. He commented on my blog where I revealed my dyslexic and right-brained traits. "That explains a lot about you back then," he wrote me. Curious, I clicked back, "How?" He answered, "I remember you said your philosophy of ministry was to light fires under people. I said mine was to put them out! Between us, we sure kept people guessing."

My friend's recollection from four decades ago illustrates two dimensions of ministry and leadership, though I'd forgotten the conversation. Any pastor who's motivated to challenge the status quo will always struggle with how much to initiate change and how much to pull back.

Many good pastoral leadership resources are out there for motivating congregations and stretching their vision. Appreciative Inquiry (AI) offers a grassroots process that elicits and affirms the best of what's happening in an organization. AI then builds on unique strengths while calling people to dream and design ways to expand and deepen those strengths.

But even with the best grassroots ownership, conflict is inevitable: healthy change and resistance are organic to creative spiritual growth. A large suburban church, using the AI process, concluded they were landlocked and needed to move to a nearby community flooded with unchurched younger people. Even with good planning, percentages of unhappy members leaving fit normal projections. However this emerging church will be different because all the pastors are engaging in spiritual guidance and weaving holistic practices into the fabric the community's life.

¡Gracias!

Open my eyes
to see the joys—
the gratitudes that rise
from suffering and surprise.

Creativity and conflict. What would be some proactive spiritual disciplines to ward off the crippling effects of backbiting church conflict? A young pastor knew before arriving that the congregation couldn't support a full time minister. After trying out various options, he and the congregation faced what might have been a head-on conflict prayerfully and realistically. They agreed for the pastor to go back to graduate school to fulfill a dream of a bi-vocational calling as a therapist and pastor. A potentially volatile situation might have caused a declining church to die. Instead it's morphed into a new model of ministry—at least for now. But then all ministry is interim. As one pastor put it, "Jesus was the intentional interim."

Even "good" surprises can morph into traumatic, life-shattering crises. Devastating conflict erupted in my fourth year at the historic parish where I expected to retire; we had bought grave plots in the pre-colonial cemetery. With an average of 70 new members joining annually over five years, homesteaders and pioneers felt scrunched behind little doors on the pews. When the anxiety exploded, we engaged a nationally recommended organizational consultant. However, I was ill equipped on a spiritual plane.

Without a single class on prayer or the spiritual life in five years at two seminaries, I knew nothing of contemplative prayer. All I knew was saying words to God, but mine were empty. I was drowning in a cauldron of conflict, yet no committee on ministry officer ever asked or coached me about Spiritual Practices. Miraculously, the dark night of leaving that parish birthed a new pulpit and a new congregation through my writing, retreat ministry, spiritual companioning—and seminary teaching. To prepare for surprise U-turns and dead ends, I offer a summary of "Seven Spiritual Strategies for Pastoral Crises."[24]

1. *Deepen your own inner life.* Exterior ferment always bids us to mine the interior life: practice examen, centering prayer, journaling, lectio in all of life.
2. *Engage in spiritual direction.* I didn't know of this ancient art. I quip, "All I knew was seeing a shrink or having a beer with a buddy." Here's something in between.
3. *Retreat to listen to your heart.* During one of my soul's darkest nights, I lived only two miles from an Abbey near Philadelphia, yet it never dawned on me to stop to pray and sort things out. I might still have left that parish, but left a bit more healed.

4. *Find or found a colleague group.* Here's one practice I followed in my 20 years of parish ministry—and still follow today. I credit these peer groups for saving my ministry—although it took a different form since 1987. (See Resource Two.)

5. *Draw on liturgical spirituality.* Our liturgies can help us pray when things are going so well that we're endangered. "When we are strong, Lord, leave us not alone; our refuge be," runs a stanza from a Presbyterian hymn, "God of Our Life." "Shield the joyous," reads a line from the Episcopal *Book of Common Prayer.* Those of us with a bipolar mindset know the danger of success without the process of discernment.

6. *Listen to your dreams.* I speak of "dreaming awake" as paying attention to your passion—to dreams of what would really be life giving; to sleep dreams; and to luminous moments in waking hours. Converse about them with a spiritual guide.

7. *Practice discernment.* In *The Spiritual Exercises,* Ignatius of Loyola offers a personal holistic process of discernment, integrating intellect and imagination, emotion and will.[25] The Quaker "Clearness Committee" provides a communal model of discernment (see Spiritual Practice 11).

Can such practices make a difference? A pastor tells of entering on a weekday afternoon the room where the church board would meet that night to vote on a controversial building program that could split the church. Chair by chair he sat, visualizing and praying for each elder. (These were Presbyterians, so he was sure where each one would sit!) For over an hour he prayed in solitude, at the same time being in community. During that night's meeting, all sensed an amazing quality of Presence—with concern for the building in relation to the people and the world.

Mini-surprises: training for mega-surprises. Small moments catch us off-balance, like the pastor who tells of being interrupted while leading his first funeral: a freaked-out mourner walked up and placed a bottle of Wild Turkey bourbon in the casket as a tribute to the deceased! The way we respond to mini-surprises trains us for the mega-surprises when we get "caught up and pounded and dazzled and astonished and beaten and broken and rescued and illuminated and rewarded and humbled." Whether wading into the bubble or the rubble of surprise we can connect with the spiritual dimension of the child and respond creatively.

SPIRITUAL PRACTICE 11: THE CLEARNESS COMMITTEE

Originally developed by the Friends for discernment for marriage, the Clearness Committee is adapted now for individuals facing a variety of vocational or life struggles. The "focus person," the one seeking clearness, chooses five or six trusted persons from various contexts of life. The focus person then writes up his or her issue (three to five pages) in advance and circulates it to the group, asking one who is prayerful to serve as convener, another as note taker. The meeting begins with silence and prayer, then a fresh statement of the concern by the focus person. This is followed by silence, then by honest, open questions ("Have you ever felt this way before?) but not advice ("Why don't you...? or "That happened to me...) All is in a prayerful, confidential atmosphere, and may end with prayer and/or the laying on of hands. The group may be reconvened. The person's life mission statement may be included as data for reflection with a Clearness Committee.

See resources by Parker Palmer (bibliography) and web link.[26] http://www.couragerenewal.org/parker/writings/clearness-committee

FOR PERSONAL REFLECTION OR GROUP CONVERSATION

1. When have you experienced pure serendipity, spontaneous joy? What are its qualities?
2. How do you perceive the relationship between church conflict and spiritual practices?
3. What's your experience with denominational leadership encouraging spiritual practices for pastors and churches in conflict? What barriers can get in the way?

12
The Digital Divide: Exchanging Wisdom across Generations

Many, many ... have been just as troubled morally and spiritually as you are right now .... You'll learn from them — if you want to. Just as some day, if you have something to offer, someone will learn something from you. It's a beautiful reciprocal arrangement.

—J.D. Salinger

When my son was in his twenties, I enlisted him to help me learn the complexities of a new computer. Sitting next to me, he noticed the anxiousness and impatience in my voice, and I realized there was more going on than my anxiety about a computer. I heard his crisp words: "Just relax. Don't panic, Dad. One thing at a time." I had an instant flashback: *I'm seeing myself, as clearly as yesterday, next to my son on the front seat of my car, saying those same words to him as he clutches, shifts, and brakes, anxiously learning to operate a stick shift transmission, just as his two older sisters had done before him.*

Could this moment of frustration morph into a moment of intimacy? I paused, recalling how my own father would pull back in such tense moments. Could I discover a new dimension to this craft of fathering in my fifties? I found myself telling my son of the flashback. We laughed and embraced. Then we proceeded with the task.

When is the younger the elder? So quickly the apprentice-mentor role reverses itself. No one has ever been an elder in the twenty-first century. So we cannot say, "This is how it is in your twenties," because no elder was ever a youth in the twenty-first century.

When life expectancy was only 35, midlife began at puberty—imagine that! You were an elder in your teens. You were still getting into mischief. Look at Jacob and Esau tricking each other and Jacob deceiving his dying father Isaac to get his brother's blessing. Youthful "pilgrims" rebelled against their parents by leaving Europe for the Americas in the 1600s. Recently, Zimbabwe was reported to have the world's lowest life expectancy—34 for men and 37 for women.

Let's say "midlife" is still the time for becoming an elder. But what is midlife in the twenty-first century in Western countries? If 70 is the new 50, is 50 the new 30? Or is it the other way around: is 20 the new 40—younger mentoring older in understanding pop culture and high-tech worlds of iPods, mp3s, blogs and texting? What if we turn such questions on their head? When is the younger the elder?

However, this is not just about elders learning from techies. A 17-year-old in a refugee camp, whose parents died of AIDS, is now in charge of the care for her three remaining younger siblings. I call that young woman an *elder in experience*. I would be awed in her presence and learn from her experience of suffering.

When the teacher is ready. The paradox of being an elder today invites us to a new paradigm of a mutual exchange of wisdom: mentoring *and* being mentored by younger generations, who are the "natives" in a changed world.

No longer can elders pour wisdom into the lives of the young. Rather, a wise elder discovers creative ways to connect and learn with younger journeyers as together we explore issues across cultures.

"When the pupil is ready, the teacher will appear," runs the ancient proverb. But try turning it on its head: "When the teacher is ready, the pupil will appear." It works both ways. If you befriend your own inner questionings as an edge of growth, you may be amazed at how seekers will appear on your doorstep as your teachers.

I say to those *over* forty, create safe spaces for listening with youthful seekers and it will be life-giving for you. I say to those *under* forty, lots of dislocated older folks would treasure a safe youthful mentor to converse with and learn from. I say to *both*, cultivate ways to connect with the struggles and questions within yourself then you will be a safe person for any yearning soul.

The digital divide in four generations. A teacher tells me of preschool children who explain to their parents how to activate the parental controls for the child's computer!

A totally new cultural phenomenon has occurred in our time that makes today's demographics unprecedented: four generations are living and working together simultaneously. In their groundbreaking book *When Generations Collide,* Baby Boomer Lynne Lancaster and Generation Xer David Stillman describe these four generations and show their clashes and gifts as they interact in the workplace.

I've adapted Lancaster and Stillman's four categories, although their generalizations invite lots of crisscrossing, especially across layers of races and cultures. By eavesdropping on their conversations we can gain powerful insights into mutual mentoring for our families and religious communities.

Traditionalists (1900-45) place their greatest value on loyalty and tend to express their allegiance in commitment to a *lifetime* career: "the legacy of a job well done." You may save up your vacation for extra retirement income; family and self-care often come in a poor second to work, making it hard to understand the Xer and Millennial mindset.

Boomers (1946-1964) value success and achievement, expressed in pursuing an *outstanding* career: "money, title, the corner office." Boomers, like their traditionalist elders, value task over relationships, while making connections for a promotion.

Generation X (1965-80) value relationships over the boss's approval and choose *portable* careers based relational concerns: "Freedom and adaptability, work in Chicago from L.A." "Everybody's in this together" explains an Xer's faux pas of failing to alphabetize the team names in email memo. Instant Boomer reaction: "Insulting! So-and-so spent decades getting to be manager, only to see some new guy's name ahead of his."

Millennials (1981-1999) value meaning with a sense of purpose and they adapt *parallel* careers: "Multitasking work that has meaning for me." Millennials take on several projects simultaneously that tap their passion and purpose. And they value process over finished product. For example, in the movie *The Social Network,* business-minded Eduardo Saverin explodes at Mark Zuckerberg about the sluggishness of Facebook project, "So when will be it finished?" Zuckerberg says, "It won't be finished. That's the point. The way fashion's never finished." One of the things my task-driven generation learns from the tech generation is that life often does not have a finish line; several major projects may be developing simultaneously. (Kierkegaard worked that way with his writing projects.)

This description of the generational puzzle provides a laboratory for learning for spiritual seekers and religious leaders. For purposes of *Clergy Table Talk,* I'll refer to these as "older generations" and "younger generations." Many Generation Xers along with their younger millennial siblings grew up as natives in the new digital landscape: they view the smart phone with its apps in their hand as an extension of their body. This description also fits the newest Generation Z, who exhibit mostly the same tech-generation characteristics of Millennials.

The real generational crisis: radical opportunity. Everyone knows mainline churches (yes, even Southern Baptists according to Diana Butler Bass) face a demographic crisis. But I say statistical extinction is not the issue. Rather, it's a spiritual crisis. The problem is not whether church as we know it exist in the 22nd century. Rather the crisis is that my generations are missing out on God's work in our lives by failing to welcome new generations as our teachers. I must intentionally draw on my Christian roots as we explore.

From modern to postmodern to primodern. Compare the traditionalist "slug-it-out, back-to-the-daily grind" work ethic to younger generations' value of relationships, and spontaneity in work that has meaning and purpose. Can we integrate older generations' value of lifelong commitment and rational concepts (modernity) with the spontaneity and portability of the younger generations (postmodernity)? I call it primodern, because it integrates our modern learnings with our primal yearnings (see Chapter 14).

From paternalism to partnership. Among younger generations there's a movement from paternalism to partnership, and understanding before acting. This fits with the idea of purpose and meaning: why would you spend good time helping people do something they don't want? Or why would you try to give people a good thing without understanding their culture first, so that indigenous leaders could interpret and implement the project?

For example, in attempting to introduce common Western vaccines in African countries, traditionalist generation leaders failed to consult the African elders. The project failed because "do good" Americans failed to explain the need and win the elder's support.

The real crisis creates a radical opportunity. In John's Gospel the *crisis* (Greek for "judgment") of the "lifting up" of the Child of Earth on the cross simultaneously refers to Jesus' exaltation as Lord of the cosmos. So in Asian languages the two characters that form the word "crisis" are composed of the words "danger" and "opportunity."

This has direct bearing on our church programs to connect with younger generations. As long as we try recruiting today's new adults just to get more support for our already existing programs, the guests will feel used by the host.

Beyond the workplace, our worship places can provide a safe, unique laboratory for learning in today's generational crisis. What other institution has the potential for mining the spiritual reciprocity of learning from each other from preschool through retirement?

Obstacles to mutual mentoring. If the reciprocity of learning among generations is important, then what are some of the obstacles that keep us from investing in each other?

Preconceived stereotypes. Not all youth are restless or socially concerned, and not all elders are tradition-bound prigs. Some youth (especially among generation Z) are more conservative than their elders, politically or theologically. Many elders, who "played it safe" in working years for the sake of career or family, now feel they've got nothing to lose by getting politically active in later years. I value cultivating a few edgy friendships on the cultural right as I do edgy friendships on the left.

Fear of being perceived as patronizing. "Most elders I know back off, or at least don't risk trying to relate to young adults, because they don't want to be perceived as patronizing or paternalistic. And, honestly, I don't know a lot of youth who feel it's worth taking their time to connect with elders," a midlife parent told me.

Fear of being perceived as dumb. "A barrier for me in connecting with younger people," said a 72-yearold woman, "is fear of showing how little I know." Maturing as an elder does not mean achieving perfection; that would turn off young generations. Rather, it means being real. Tech generations are not care if God exists. Rather is God real? The same goes for any relationship: Is this person real?

Being real eclipses traditionalist arguments about gender, sexual, and racial identity. A 20-something pastor said, "For most of my generation, the 'gay' issue is a non-issue." Rather, they're looking for spiritual integrity and transparency.

A multigenerational team was meeting with their new department director, an African American, as Lancaster and Stillman tell it. "As the employees were getting to know their new boss, the Generation Xer piped up: 'I'm never sure what the right terminology is. Do you consider yourself black, African American, or a person of color?'" Traditionalists and Boomers were stunned and embarrassed. "To their relief, the African American boss actually *thanked* the Xer and gave a thoughtful response."[27] Older generations' fear of lawsuits, coupled with looking stupid, made talk about diversity a thing to avoid rather than learn from. The story leads into the paradox integrating the transparent spontaneity of youth with the serious lifelong commitment of elders.

Playful yet serious: the youth in the elder, the elder in the youth. When Adam Werbach was the youngest-ever president of the Sierra Club at age 23, he related "a cautionary tale for our times." Researchers, he reported, went to a preschool and asked the youngsters, "Who knows how to sing?" Everyone's hand shot up. "Who knows how to dance?" They waved their hands. "Who knows how to draw?" Again, all hands up. Fast forward a week and the researchers posed the questions to college students. "Who knows how to sing?" A few hands were raised. "Who knows how to dance?" Two hands went up halfway. "Draw?" No response.

Somewhere between preschool and so-called "higher" education we lose track of a vital means of self-expression. No wonder—pun intended!—we resort to violence. Dancing, drumming, drawing, and dreaming get squeezed out of us.

To advance spiritually means returning to a childlike habit of mind in all religious traditions. "The great person is one who does not lose the child's heart," writes Confucian leader Mencius in the third century B.C.E.[28] When Jesus tells a Jewish teacher Nicodemus that "to see" the realm of God he must be born again, Nicodemus takes Jesus literally: "Can one enter a second time into the mother's womb and be born?"[29] The Sufi Muslim poet Hafiz asks God to "take care of that / Holy infant my heart has become."[30]

We can create playful projects for serious purposes. "The best scientists are those who retain the somewhat naïve curiosity of a child," says Margaret Geller, chief scientist at the Smithsonian Astrological Observatory. "They see the world with a special eye."[31]

Children

We are children first,
    then try feverishly
        to become adults,
      until painfully
we become children again.
        And again...

Paradigm: the youthful Jesus teaching the elders. The Luke's Gospel offers an archetype of the "the elder in the youth." Jesus, at age twelve, worries his parents sick that he's lost in the crowd. "After three days, they find him in the temple among the teachers, listening to them and asking them questions. And all who heard him were amazed at his understanding and his answers" (Luke 2:46-47). The story is a paradigm of the Jungian dream archetype of "the precocious child," pointing to why scientists often make discoveries in a playful, spontaneous moment. The story is also a paradigm of how listening to stories and asking questions act as a shuttle to weave our conscious and unconscious selves together, and to connect the generations.

In *Mozart's Brain and the Fighter Pilot,* Richard Restak says, "You can enhance your creativity by playfully altering your perceptions and trying to look beyond the obvious, most practical interpretations of what you see around you."[32]

Alexander Fleming's lazy lab students, by neglecting to clean the moldy Petri dishes, became his unwitting mentors. Fleming's surprise discovery of penicillin is still healing generations.

In young adulthood we need "guarantors of our identity," Erik Erikson says in his classic *Childhood and Society.* In later years we need to experience "generativity" by conferring that kind of identity and self-reliance on younger people. What if it works a bit both ways? Is that not a beautiful reciprocal arrangement?

SPIRITUAL PRACTICE 12. CONTEMPLATING QUALITIES OF A CHILD

Find the lyrics to the child's lullaby "Hush Little Baby" (don't you cry). Or listen to Yo-Yo Ma and Bobby McFerrin's version on their CD *Hush* as they have fun, counterpointing classic 'cello and pop styles. Have pen and paper ready. Pause. Contemplate childlike qualities. Begin to write words, phrases or images of childlike qualities—or draw smiley faces, sad faces, or stick figures jumping, kneeling, or dancing. You might let a poem emerge. Find a way to name these childlike qualities with another person or in a group.

FOR PERSONAL REFLECTION OR GROUP CONVERSATION

1. From the above exercise, what childlike qualities come to your mind?
2. Did you think of "positive" qualities, like curiosity or trust? Were any "negative," like impatience or tantrums? What about "holy" impatience or "creative" anger?
3. Assess your relationships across the four generations. Recall and meditate on an experience when you clashed with another generation member. Then recall and meditate on an experience when you learned from a member of another generation. Find a way to converse about these experiences with someone.

13

Issues Clergy
Don't Talk About:
Internet Addictions
and Integrity

This above all: to thine own self be true,
And it must follow, as the night the day,
Thou canst not then be false to any man.
—William Shakespeare

Struggle changes us; it grows us up. Struggle is the
midwife of transformation.
—Joan D. Chittister

"All of us here are pretty much eclectic," the speaker said,
alluding to varied spiritual traditions such as Benedictine, Ignatian,
Quaker, Buddhist or Hindu. But in an instant, I thought, "No, not
eclectic—integrative!" At break time I was conversing with another
participant who had the same thought: "How do these two sound
different?"

Integrity: the core of "who I am." I've raised this question
with friends over dinner, strangers at airports, and companions in
spiritual direction: How does *eclectic* sound different from *integrative?*
One said, "Well, eclectic sounds like dabbling, take a bit from here,
from there, depending on what works, what feels good." Another
said, "Eclectic seems like drawing from the surface; integrative
connects with the core of who you are." The speaker was right:
American culture, secular and spiritual, is largely eclectic.

Integrating life's gifts and struggles in a daily examen leads to integrity.

In a presentation on the emotional, physical and spiritual benefits of exercise, a slide showed a huge sign over a modern recreation center, with lots of steps leading up to the entrance. But all the people entering the rec center were riding up the outdoor escalator! Instead of compartmentalizing actions and intentions, integrity means incorporating exercises—spiritual and physical—into the whole of life.

Integrity is not a thing you can grab and put in your pocket. Rather, love is as love does. A person of integrity, then, is one who practices a continual habit of discernment. When confronted with impromptu choices, a person of integrity asks, what decision aligns best with who I am? Which choice would keep me true to the core of my soul, to my unique life and experience of God? "This above all: to thine own self be true" (Shakespeare, *Hamlet* I.ii.78).

Internet threats to clergy integrity. Internet technology, like all created things, offers incredible creative and destructive potential. Two incendiary threats of the Internet culture are throwing many clergy wildly off course: addiction to online pornography and plagiarizing.

How can spiritual leaders in this exploding Internet culture avoid selling our souls and stay true to our core? In a word, how can you practice integrity?

Story one. Jeremy felt a roller coaster of emotions in a matter of moments. There was excitement at searching through the scores of erotic pictures that flashed on his computer screen; the thrill of climax; and then shame at having done all of this in his church office. Suddenly, he heard someone at the door. He panicked. His heart was racing. Had he remembered to lock it? As the doorknob jangled but did not budge, Jeremy felt fear give way to relief. He expressed sincere thanks to God for having dodged a potentially disastrous encounter and wholeheartedly vowed to never do it again. But two months later, after a particularly tense finance meeting in which people seemed to imply that he was responsible for the decline in giving, Jeremy retreated to his office, booted up his computer, and sought his escape.[33]

Story two. In a New York *Times* article, a high-profile minister admitted plagiarizing sermons Sunday after Sunday. "It's a pattern you get into," the pastor said, explaining personal struggles at the time with issues of self-esteem. "It happens bit by bit. You end up using more and more. You're using a little material maybe initially, and then using more. It's really not rational."[34]

Each pastor's story has things in common: the subtle strangulation process of online addictions; the element of stealing (time from church for pornography; another's words with plagiarism); the secret duplicity of false pretenses; the resulting shame.

But there are differences: centuries before the Internet, honorable preachers have quoted and used other's sermons, giving proper credit. It's a matter of degree and honesty. Yet I recall with sadness a pastor resigning with a confession that many of his sermons were taken from the Internet. I also recall a younger pastor confiding that he had actually written a sermon of his own; I encouraged him to mine the unique gifts of grace in his own vulnerable soul. Integrity is still the watchword.

Integrity is a lifelong fruit of a day-by-day process of integrating your life with your experience of God. The goal: being authentic, even vulnerable. It's a movement through perfectionism and pretense to being real. It's about living into the transforming Mystery, at the same time turning to Reality.

Online porn addiction. Let's listen in on the biggest issue clergy don't talk about.

In their online article "The Pastor and Pornography," Mark Sundby, executive director of North Central Ministry Development Center and Susan Nienaber, Senior Consultant for The Alban Institute, say that 70% of the U.S. population regularly use porn, and a third to over half of pastors admit they use Internet pornography, including evangelical pastors. They ask, if it's so natural, why should we be concerned? It's an excellent question, and I paraphrase the authors' three good reasons to take pornography use seriously.[35]

First, on a societal level, sex addiction experts have deemed the burgeoning porn crisis "our newest and most challenging mental health problem. Many men don't see this dizzying proliferation of online services as forms of prostitution."[36] Perhaps even more concerning, the largest users of pornography are among those who attend our church youth groups, ages 13 to 17. As moral leaders, many pastors know that they should speak out, but cannot in good conscience when they're accessing the same material.

Second, on a personal level, numerous pastors have crossed the line from occasional to frequent use of Internet pornography. Addicted clergy spend hours each week searching the web, take risks by accessing it in church offices, set aside ministry tasks in favor of the sexual high, and damage their personal lives by neglecting spouses, family, and friends. Meeting with a therapist can help a pastor figure out where they are on a continuum, as with other issues, and identify strategies to address it so that they can continue to flourish in ministry. Not addressing it can lead to devastating outcomes.

Third, on a congregational level, the fallout varies when a pastor is caught using Internet pornography on a church computer. As with other types of sexual misconduct, many folks feel deeply betrayed. The way the pastor, congregational leaders, and denominational officials respond can make a world of difference for the clergyperson's future and the congregation's ability to recover in a healthy manner.

Factors that put clergy at risk. What are some of the situations that make clergy susceptible to online addictions? With each, can you brainstorm your own ways to counteract the liability with a positive behavioral strategy?

Isolation and lack of close friends. I recall Bruce Larson once writing a powerful piece, "How are you fixed for friends?" One of the goals of this little book is to provide a catalyst for colleague support and accountability groups (see Resource Two).

Unstructured time; working and studying alone. You might draft a tentative schedule each week with time blocks for various tasks to provide a healthy self-structure.

Expectations of "the ideal pastor" that foster shame. Creative ways to debunk "the pastor pedestal" can foster transparency. I used to share with my elders a "for instance" of a cancelled meeting: how would they suggest I use the time? Catch up on reading? Prayer? Spend it with family? Visit a homebound member? Play the piano? Do a woodworking project? It caused some discomfort, but it created a real-life, not an abstract, process.

Reluctance for church board to address the issues. It behooves the pastor to bring up the subject to the board for guidelines for sexual conduct, including Internet concerns.

The set of the sail: healthy spiritual perspectives. If there's any one thing I learned from my late mentor Gerald May, a psychiatrist and a spiritual director at Shalem Institute, it's this: we are destined for freedom but each of us is addicted to stuff. "Addiction holds us back from our rightful destiny," May writes in Addiction and Grace. But grace is two-sided: "The power of grace flows most fully when human will chooses to act in harmony with divine will.... It is the difference between testing God by avoiding one's own responsibilities and trusting God as one acts responsibly."[37]

My brushes with lethal addictions are as real as anyone's, but so is my experience of practicing grace in the grit, as I convey in this poem.

Addictions

> To being late,
> and looking great,
> success and sex
> and youthfulness,
> to action, motion,
> foolish notions,
> Internet, people,

shirking, working,
skin and kin:

Kyrie eleison,
Christe eleison,
Kyrie eleison.
Lord have mercy,
Christ have mercy,
Lord have mercy.

I move from shaming
myself to naming
the demons to claiming
my true identity:

I am who I am.

We can look for transforming gifts in the wildest Internet struggles. Joan Chittister writes in *Scarred by Struggle, Transformed by Hope,* "Struggle is the midwife of transformation."

Ask yourself, how can I maintain freedom to love instead of succumbing to enslaving addictions? Greet each outward distraction as an invitation to deeper inward development. Befriend your struggles and questions and the stories and patterns of your own journey. Enjoy innocent pleasures that leave no regret, no yucky residue. Seek help through a therapist, a spiritual guide, and a colleague support group—and all the above.

Struggles of others as guides to my own issues. In Eastern tradition, the guru often tells a story in answer to a question, or asks another question. Or the seeker may provoke a question in the guru.

A woman brought her daughter to Mohandas Gandhi because the child was addicted to sweets. Gandhi met with the child a few minutes, and then told the mother to bring her child back in a month. When the mother returned, again Gandhi met with the child a few minutes, then told the mother she could go home. Amazingly, the girl broke with her addiction to sweets. The mother, curious about what had happened, returned to Gandhi yet a third time to ask, why did he not say to her daughter at first whatever he must have said the second time? Gandhi replied that he himself had been addicted to sweets and could not offer a true word to her until he was free.

When Arun Gandhi tells this story about his grandfather, he makes the point that the elder Mahatma was "great" because he could allow "the least of these" to call his own life into question.[38] A young person's problem became the teacher for the elder. Authentic mentoring happens when the seeker and teacher are both transformed in the encounter. And it saves us from paternalism. Is this not a message to spiritual leaders to welcome the gift in the questions of seekers who cross our paths?

SPIRITUAL PRACTICE 13. THE GIFT OF THE STRUGGLE

I invite you to visualize some aspect of your life where you are presently struggling to be free. Then, picture yourself acting as if you simply gave up on the struggle. Let this be a call to renew your commitment to the *gift* of the struggle. (Suggested meditations: Mark 1:35-38; Romans 13:12-14; Colossians 1:29.)

FOR PERSONAL REFLECTION OR GROUP CONVERSATION

1. "No, not eclectic—integrative!" The author asks, "How do they sound different?"
2. "When confronted with impromptu choices, a person of integrity asks, what decision aligns best with who I am? Which choice would keep me true to the core of my soul, to my unique life and experience of God?" What gets in the way of your making choices true to the core of who you are?
3. When has another person's struggle become a gift to some issue in your life?

14

Postmodern to Primodern: Preaching after the Jesus Seminar

Truth is truth, whether from the lips of Jesus or Balaam.
—George McDonald

Thus we clutch a momentary intimacy in worship when we become momentarily a part of a larger whole, a fleeting strength, which we pit against all the darkness and dread of other times.
—Howard Thurman

Fred Craddock, a preacher's preacher, is a master at retelling a biblical story in such a way that he doesn't need to import jokes; he lifts up humor within the story itself. After retelling the story of the wasted Prodigal who returns home—with the stew of emotions as the father throws him a party, with the unseen mother masterminding the whole thing, with the older sibling exploding, with the neighbors watching this dysfunctional family—Craddock ended with a question: "Would you have come to the party?"

I never forgot the question. Rabbi Jesus often left people with a Zen-like question or parable to get them buzzing. Why not end more sermons with a question, or a riddle, to sharpen the eye for the journey, to haunt the imagination, to deepen the Mystery?

A new kind of faith: passionate yet open. I'm calling for a new kind of faith—*passionate for love yet open to question*. It's a call to integrate *critical thinking with contemplative living*. It's about how to preach passionately on Christmas Eve after you and some of your lay leaders have read Marcus Borg and John Dominic Crossan's *The*

First Christmas—and you're saying what shepherds, what angels, what magi? I choose to call this new quest "primodern," because it seeks to unite our primal yearnings with modern learnings. Four cultural mindsets can generate a primodern spirituality that's passionate yet open.

Primal oral. Here spirituality is still passed down primarily through stories and music, rituals and gestures, and memorizable proverbs or koans. One still encounters oral culture today in "third world" countries, but also in rural regions and ethnic areas of so-called "developed" countries, with many correlations to pop culture.

Literal fundamentalist. Rigid belief systems, in religious or secular guises, freeze their founder's original ideas. A little doctrine set in stone is a dangerous thing. *Isms* paralyze the soul. Fundamental*ism* ignites hate and turns thinking people away from faith; still in an anxious age people get drawn to it. Yet basic "fundamentals" are good if used as foundation stones for building, not rocks for hurling.

Modern rational. The Enlightenment era spawned individual creativity, analytical thinking and democratic ideals. But sadly reason displaced both the mythical and mystical. Theological education has been heavy on the *logical* and light on *theo*: in the 1960s we demythologized the Gospels, and the mystics were deemed irrelevant in my training.

Yet I value modern critical scientific and literary tools; they help us take an intellectually honest look at sources of faith. For example, I value the work of the popular "Jesus Seminar": What did Jesus *really* say and do? Picking up on Albert Schweitzer's classic, *The Quest of the Historical Jesus*, Borg and Crossan and company opened up this 19th century quest for 21st century disciples. But after stripping away layers added by the early Gospel editors, how do you make sense of the "skinny" Jesus of history—and journey into the Christ of experience?

Postmodern. Enter postmodern thought, which can hold opposites like rational thinking and spontaneous experience in creative paradox. In his bestseller, The Elegant Universe: Superstrings, Hidden Dimensions, and the Quest for the Ultimate Theory, Brian Greene describes his amazing T.O.E. (Theory Of Everything) for "lay" folks like me: "From one principle—that everything at its most microscopic level consists of combinations of vibrating strands—string theory provides a single explanatory framework capable of encompassing all forces and all matter."[39] T.O.E. can take seemingly contradictory theories—Newton's gravity and Einstein's $E=MC^2$ and Heisenberg's "uncertainty principle"—and wrap them in one big bundle. So postmodern thought espouses mystery, and each solution begs a new question. This is the upside of postmodernism.

But downside of postmodern thought is loneliness and fragmentation. If everything is relative without "absolute" truth, it's hard to develop community without common beliefs. Can we forge a new kind of compassionate contemplative community, where each blind person gains respect for the others' descriptions of their part of the elephant?

Enter primodern: high-tech, high-touch. "Postmodern" sounds as if we somehow moved beyond modernity and reason. Really? Are you reading this book? Do you use a computer? That's why I'm proposing a new term *primodern,* with its goal to integrate our primal knowing with modern knowledge.

Primal cultures have many similarities to modern high-tech culture. Sound-bite communications, like primal parables and riddles, work well for many of us with ADHD (Attention Deficit Hyperactive Disorder) or dyslexic tendencies. Primal symbols and stories, gestures and art, metaphors and music, bridge all four generations (see Chapter 12). In this kind of preaching and worship, you provide an immediacy of experience for today's tech set *and* their nonagenarian elders with short-term memory loss.

Primodern culture can wed the most advanced theories of science or politics or theology with the innocent wonder of a child. Primodern baptizes modern and primal: high-tech, high-touch.[40] Cool computer screens and impersonal systems leave tech generations starved for spiritual intimacy in genuine community. Here's the church's golden prospect.

Here's a practical high-tech, high-touch idea. Using a large movie house screen in worship, for many churches causes a digital divide not only between generations, but also between mindsets within generations. What to do? At St. John's Cathedral in Denver, Colorado, instead of a drop-down movie screen that would clash with the gothic architecture, they often suspend a gauze muslin-textured drape. On this subtle cloth are projected slides of traditional Russian icons, scenes of Denver or ancient Israel and Palestine—or an occasional quote or DVD clip can be shown as part of the homily.

From de-mything to re-mything: Primodern perspectives can help our quest to reinvigorate ancient texts. Instead of simplistic either/or categories that divide people, the paradox of primal and modern can hold differences in both/and creative tension.

Primoderns can return to primal language like "down" and "up" *as metaphor*, letting the immediacy of experience stand side by side with rational facts and ideas.

Instead of demything miracle stories and fairy tales as "silly," we can re-myth them, connecting ancient poetic truth with fragmented narratives of our own lives.

"Up and Down": Everest and a "Second Naiveté." Bishop John Shelby Spong tells how the late space scientist Carl Sagan humorously "proved" that Jesus could not have "ascended to heaven" in scientific terms. Given two thousand years, by Sagan's calculations, Jesus would still be zooming through a nearby galaxy![41] So the myth of Jesus' ascension seems to be a relic from ancients who pictured God as "up" in the heavens, closer in mountaintops and thunderstorms. Moderns, who know all about travel in outer space, cannot stomach such "facts." Where is up? Or down?

Yet folks go right on using the language of "up" and "down." This is what Paul Ricoeur meant by a "second naïveté."[42] We can return to childhood terms in our preaching, but use them poetically, not literally. The computer is down. Downsizing does not mean shrinking the corporate office building or the person fired. As I take my morning walk, I find myself singing lines of an African American spiritual: "Nobody knows the trouble I've seen, nobody knows my sorrow, Glory! Hallelujah! Sometimes I'm up, sometimes I'm down... Sometimes I'm almost to the ground, O yes Lord." For many, like me, who live with bipolar disorder, the up-down images, counterpointing sorrow and glory, bless our wild emotional swings.

When preaching about these concepts like these, why not break out singing a spiritual song such as this (gesturing for others to join), so that people *experience* right then and there the reality of the idea you're communicating?

Modernity tried to steal our myths. We smile at primal peoples who still think God is closer on a mountain. Yet why do sophisticated Americans go trekking to the Catskills of upstate New York? An I-Max movie portrays the climbers' lure for Mt. Everest. The tremendous mystery that saves Everest's climbers is daring courage *and* holy fear. If you ever lose the fear, you're dead. Maybe we're all more primal than we thought.

Primodern: grown-up *and* childlike. When I was young, my mother confided in me that my grandmother Maime thought "the sun rose and set on Woodrow Wilson"—a Democrat in my Republican family! I knew exactly what the metaphor meant—though I also knew the sun is actually a star, and it's the earth that moves so the sun does not rise or set—nor had President Wilson got sunburned in its rays.

What is the difference between personifying God: "The sound of the Lord God walking in the garden in the cool of the day"—or the stock market: "Wall Street got nervous at the sound of saber rattling"? A reporter tells us that "Oil" has enough votes for drilling Alaskan reserves, and we understand that indigenous people's pleas to save the caribou do not have a chance. Wall Street's sidewalks do not have nerve endings; my car's oil does not vote. Metaphors allow us to be grown-up and naïve at the same time.

I tell my New England cousin that I'll "walk" with him through a major vocational transition, but I do not mean I'll develop huge legs that straddle all the way from Colorado to New Hampshire. In the same way I can say God has "walked" with me through many dangers, toils and snares. It is a very personal walk, but God does not need feet and toes. "Walk" embodies Paul Riceour's "second naiveté": my *personal* "walk with God" and my *ethical* life in the world: "Walk the talk."

So can we integrate older generations' value of lifelong commitment and rational concepts (modernity) with the spontaneity and portability of the younger generations (postmodernity)? It's called primodern spirituality, serious yet playful.

Facts and Truth: Paradox and Process. A monk who had lived in Rwanda told me of a decades-old dispute between two groups. When a new chief called a council, a man stood up and began "putting the facts straight," rehearsing the same old grievances—dates, names, atrocities. The chief interrupted, "We're not here to restate the facts, but to find a solution that embodies a truth we can all live with."

Here is primodern leadership: translate this to church conflict. You realize how experience skews the facts, therefore pursuing "truth" is a process of finding life-giving goals while living with unresolved points of view.

Resiliency: resurrection as experience. Metaphor and story weave truths with facts. A woman got help for her intellectual quest from Japanese novelist Shusako Endo's *A Life of Jesus*. Endo distinguishes between truth and fact. The timeless truth of the gospel—that Love bounces back—can absorb the wildest scholarly guesses about the facts of Jesus' empty tomb.

Once, just as I was ready to lead a retreat, a physician asked, "What do you think really happened on Easter?" I confessed not knowing in *fact* what happened to Jesus' physical body. Nevertheless, for me the empty tomb stories in the Gospels are *real*. It is women, like Mary Magdalene (my intuitive self), who have the courage to go to the tomb and encounter its dark emptiness. When Mary tells the men (my practical self), they go back home to fishing. But she stays on and weeps. So, I said, I have lingered and leaned into that empty darkness.

Then, as sad and scared as Mary, I turn outward to see Jesus anonymously, *incognito,* as the gardener—as a stranger on the road, an advice-giving fisher, a chef on the shore—as the least of these. That, I said, is what resurrection means: *we journey alongside the Jesus of history into the Christ of experience.* Jesus keeps showing up, but what if I don't speak to the gardener?

Primoderns can simultaneously question "facts" of history and still experience the "truth" it bears. T.S. Eliot muses on this tension: "The hint half guessed, the gift half understood, is / Incarnation."[43] Paradox embraces this doubting believing tension. To recast Luther's saying, "Sin boldly, but believe more boldly still," I say, Doubt boldly; but love more boldly still.

Questioning and storying the sermon. One of the sad things about much of today's preaching is that it's so cerebral and disconnected to people's burning issues, or the issues that ought to be burning. To begin by raising a real-life question, or by telling a story followed by a question, gets people on board. When preaching on one of Jesus' parables, it's so easy to slide into a left-brain sermon and spoil a right-brain story.

Ask instead: How can I reinvent the biblical story—or connect with a fresh story of my own experience—in a way that comes alive so the listener sees oneself in it? I call this "storying the sermon": fleshing out the ideas with lived experiences. The word needs to become flesh, or we have a disembodied worship.

I also talk about "questioning" the sermon in the same way a good writer anticipates questions in the reader. Go through the manuscript, and convert a couple of your best insights into questions. Confess your own misgivings about how Jesus could literally walk on water. Then disclose a harrowing experience where you (or someone else) "walked on water" in a difficult time.

The skinny Jesus. What's left of the "skinny Jesus" after the Jesus Seminar? I'd say it's pretty powerful: it's about compassion. To paraphrase a line from Harper Lee's *To Kill a Mocking Bird,* "It's

about love getting inside people's skin and walking around in it."
You can preach for life on that. The Christian mystery proclaims
that God has entered the stuff of this world and is present in Christ
through the Spirit to transform brokenness into blessing.

It's the truth of experience. Albert Schweitzer, who amazingly
integrated his life as a theologian, physician, musician and
philanthropist, wrote in the concluding paragraph of *The Quest of
the Historical Jesus*: "Jesus comes to us as One unknown, without a
name, as of old, by the lake-side, to those who knew not... and
speaks to us the same word: "Follow me!" ... And to those who
pay attention, whether they are wise or simple, this One will reveal
the Divine in the toils, the conflicts, and the sufferings, which they
shall pass through in this company, and, as a mystery beyond words,
they shall learn in their own experience who this One is."[44] So we
journey alongside the Jesus of history into the Christ of experience.

SPIRITUAL PRACTICE 14. A CONTEMPLATIVE SPIN ON THE GOLDEN RULE

Be attentive for occasion during this week when you feel a quick impulse to react to someone's comment or idea: *Pause.* Take a deep breath. Imagine for an instant being in their skin, inhabiting their thoughts. See if the pause affects your response.

FOR PERSONAL REFLECTION OR GROUP CONVERSATIONS

1. Ponder the author's characterization of primodern spirituality as *serious* yet *playful*. Pause and recall an example. What were the qualities of that experience?
2. When have you had the experience of love "getting inside someone else's skin?" How does that metaphor add meaning to the Golden Rule?

15

The Only Way and Many Rooms: Christian Ministry in a Pluralistic World

What can we say about the curious juxtaposition of seemingly contradictory texts? Could it be telling us about the need to hold the universal and the particular together and about the central place Jesus must have for Christians even in the most expansive interfaith dialogue?

—Harvey Cox

On his way back from Haiti, a friend tells this story about going through customs inspection. The person ahead of him had bought lots of costly jewellery, but was waved through by the customs officer with a mere glance. My friend had only an inexpensive carved head of Jesus. But it was big, about knee-high, so he had wrapped it in several layers of towels in a burlap bag. As the officer dug deeper into the towels, expecting expensive hidden items, suddenly he looked up and asked, "How big is your Jesus, anyway?"

That is *the* question for third-millennium Christians. For I am convinced the more we drink from the unique well of Christ, the more we will connect with the universal underground stream that draws all people of faith.

The Only Way? (and Many Rooms): John 14:1-6. "I am the way, and the truth, and the life. No one comes to the Father but by me." Extremists misuse this exclusive-sounding text to kill or convert people against their will. But I want to show how the text

about the "only way" and "many rooms" in John 14:1-6 is one of
the most inclusive in the Bible. Jesus may not have said these exact
words, but they echo the voice of Jesus through the community
back *then*. What do they say to us *now*?

"I am the way…No one comes to the Father except through
me." But what is the "way"? And who is the "me" that is the *only*
way? Jesus was very clear about that in Matthew 25: "Just as you
did it to one of the least of these who are members of my family,
you did it to me." During Jesus' brief ministry he went around
touching the lives of people on the edges of society: lepers and
tax collectors, filthy rich folks and beaten-down widows, prostitutes
and Roman military officials—this despite his clear pacifist
teaching.

In high-tech culture we long to touch Jesus and be touched.
We're like "doubting Thomas," who said, "Unless I see the mark
of the nails in his hands… and put my finger in his side, I will not
believe" (John 20:25). The beautiful thing is that by touching the
broken lives of "the least of these"—people with AIDS, prisoners,
dehydrated children and their starving parents—we do get to touch
the living Christ in the wounds of others.

To ignore the least of these is to miss the only way. It is the Way
of the cross, the way of dying and rising, the way of brokenness
morphing to blessing. It is as if Jesus says, "Meet me at the edges,
in the marginal people and marginal parts of yourself, for that is
the only way to see me rise at the center." It is the primal Way of
Life-giving "sacrifice at the navel of the universe" (*Rig Veda*). It is
"the Lamb slain from the foundation of the world' (Revelation
13:8, KJV). It is the *Tao Te Ching,* the "Way that has Power"—by
whatever name.

All this rings true to Jesus' Easter appearances. Jesus seems
unconcerned about name recognition: appearing in the guise of a
gardener at the tomb, a stranger on the road to Emmaus, an advice-
giving fisher on the shore. And when two disciples' eyes are opened
and they recognize Jesus in the breaking of the bread at
Emmaus—he disappears! At the tomb when Mary recognizes the

gardener is Jesus, she is told: "Do not hold on to me!" The final judgment of a true disciple is to be in touch with the least of these in genuine self-forgetting love: "Lord, when did we see you hungry...?" That is Truth.

This is what it means to be called "followers of the Way"—the way that is revealed in the *Acts* of the Apostles—the *mitzvoth* in Hebrew—the deeds that give life to the Word, and the only way worth living. That is Life.

Many Rooms? (and the Only Way): John 14:1-6. Primodern faith wants to hold together the paradox of "only way" in John 14:6 with the "many rooms" in John 14:2: "In my father's house there are many rooms." This is the voice of same Jesus who says in John 10, "I have other sheep that do not belong to this fold."

If ever there was a time when we need to think of various traditions of the Way as rooms in the world's one big house, it is now. In *The Next Christianity,* Philip Jenkins warns of new crusades, in a mix of religious and political enemies. But in *Mere Christianity* C. S. Lewis gives us the wisest of words about these many rooms: "When you have reached your own room, be kind to those who have chosen different doors and to those who are still in the hall. If they are wrong, they need your prayers all the more, and if they are your enemies, then you are under orders to pray for them. That is one of the rules common to the whole house."[45]

What Might the Church of the Way Look like in the Third Millennium? I offer a couple of story-pictures to serve as icons of hope.

People were abuzz at the adult class in an inner-city church. Police had arrested a young man for breaking in and stealing a computer from the church office. "Too bad," members complained; it was one more sign of the deteriorating neighborhood. Bud Smith, soft-spoken retiree, quietly asked had anyone been to the county jail to visit the suspected youth. After an awkward silence, Bud said he would visit the prisoner. The gesture of that single visit began a long-term relationship with the troubled neighborhood youth. Bud gained a new understanding of the inner city youth and their problems and shared his experiences and got church people involved. As neighborhood families noticed the church's changing attitude, new bridges were built between Hope church and its community.[46] The seed is concealed in a question. The power is embodied in a gesture.

Near San Diego a cross standing on public land became the cause of a big fight, as an Atheist Coalition got the permit to use it on Easter morning. Jesus would not be so concerned about that as over the hateful ways some of his disciples fought against this. However, one Christian group baked muffins and quietly served them to the atheists as they gathered that Easter dawn.[47] That is the church; there is the gospel.

Christ and Inter-Faith Spirituality. I want to speak of the Christ dimension of my personal story journey. Transforming brokenness into blessing is central to my theology and spirituality. For me, Jesus Christ is the heart of this transforming mystery. It's about resiliency, the mystery that whenever we descend to the hell of despair and rise again with compassion and gratitude, we experience the Christ. Wherever I see mysterious transforming inklings of Love at work in nature, nations or human nature—in Muslim, Jewish, Hindu or even atheist people—for me it's the Christ experience, though I don't force my language on others.

I link the Christian mystery with the Buddhist text that says the beautiful lotus grows out of the garbage; so Jesus was crucified on the town garbage heap at Golgotha and rises, beautiful, though often transparent. I can maintain my unique faith in Christ, relating it to universal spiritual meanings. The "only way" is the Way of dying to what is fake and rising to what is real, by whatever name.

SPIRITUAL PRACTICE 15: MANY ROOMS, THE ONLY WAY

Meditate with the metaphor of many rooms in God's house. Imagine entering into some of those rooms, one at a time, each inhabited by persons of a different religious tradition—children, youth, and adults. What questions do you ask? What questions do they ask you? What stories do you tell each other? What do you learn? Pause a moment. Now, imagine traveling on a road with many obstacles, surrounded with the same persons. There is no other way; to veer off on your own would be too dangerous; and you need to make your destination by nightfall. As you encounter each obstacle, what do you notice happening among the group? What common qualities emerge? Just ahead, you see a lighted house—the same house with many rooms where you began. This time, as you enter and walk past each room, what is the prayer of your heart?

FOR PERSONAL REFLECTION OR GROUP CONVERSATION

1. Reflect on Harvey Cox's question: "What can we say about the curious juxtaposition of seemingly contradictory texts?" (See John 14:2 and 6.)
2. What happens if you choose to live by mainly one or the other?
3. What does it look like to live with both in a creative tension?
4. In his book *Love Wins*, Rob Bell insists that God has a bigger job description than serving as the club bouncer who checks tickets at heaven's door. How would such a perspective affect your life mission here on this earth? (See Resource Three.)

Resource One:
Keeping a Spiritual Journal

Writing longhand in a journal taps primal images and energies, though some people journal creatively with a computer. Use your journal to reflect on conversations or events, scriptures or dreams; to practice examen (see Spiritual Practice 1); to create poetry or art. Use pastel colors. Glue things in your journal: a leaf, a feather, a friend's e-mail note, a quote or a news headline. Use sticky notes generously to jot an insight, a prayer concern, a dream fragment recalled at midday; insert them later. Log a few sections to read back to front (like the Hebrew Bible): movies you've seen, books you've read, favorite centering prayer words or phrases, quotations that nurture you, your life mission statement.

I joke about making only two rules. First, date each entry; second, make a mistake in the first one—because trying to say things right is a huge barrier. Another is missed days—so aim for four days out of seven. Probably the biggest barrier to journaling is being too self-critical, writing out of the head instead of the heart.

To break through this impasse, I suggest a simple method. From time to time, open to a clean page in your journal. Let your eye fall on an object in the room where you're sitting. Contemplate it for one minute. Then begin to write words or phrases *down* the page (instead of complete sentences from left to right). Once when I was leading a workshop in a federal prison, one man wrote:

> Air vent in ceiling, high
> like prison walls.
> Air inside confined
> mixes with
> air outside free.
> Breathing in this air, I am
> free inside.

I invite you to try this method to jumpstart your own journaling. You can use your journal for many of the spiritual practices in this little book, which are designed to link left-brain thinking and right-brain imagination.

Resource Two:
Finding or Founding a
Colleague Group

Purpose and composition. Four to seven participants commit to be present for each other as spiritual companions (usually meeting monthly) in a contemplative atmosphere for mutual support and for personal, professional and spiritual growth. Note: The sample below calls for a convener and two presenters at each meeting.

Getting started. Meet for lunch with one other person who endorses the purpose and the ground rules and who is willing to experiment with sample format, below. If the chemistry between you seems good, then each invite one other, etc., up to six.

Ground Rules. Each person commits to keep confidentiality, to refrain from advice giving, to ask only open questions, to share appropriate stories or offer non-judgmental observations, and to pray for each other. Beyond these, the group may modify the format and evaluate as they go along.

Options for presenters. First presenter (issue-focused): Using the format below, present yourself in relation to a real-life experience in ministry. Keep the focus on the question: what is the Spirit doing in the presenter's life through this incident?—not trying to "fix" a problem. Second presenter (topic-focused): Lead a book study (like Clergy Table Talk), with everyone reading a chapter or so a month; or lead a scripture lectionary study; or present a book review; or present a brief original paper.

Convener. The convener's role is to open the group with a time of contemplative prayer, followed by personal sharing; and to remind the group of the agreed-upon times and ground rules. (At the end of each meeting, choose a convener for the next time.)

Sample format. This is designed for a group of six, for about two and a half hours.

OPENING (10 MINUTES)

The convener may place an object on a table or stool: a candle, bowl, quill pen, stone, a classic book, or any symbol of writing or nature. Convener: Invite the group to five minutes of silence, opening and/or ending the silence with a brief quotation, prayer, scripture, poem, or music. After ten minutes, invite the checking in (3 or 4 minutes each).

FIRST PRESENTATION (50 MINUTES)

√ Listen without interruption as the presenter speaks (distribute copies if desired).
√ Be comfortable with silences.
√ Be attentive to one another and keep a contemplative ethos.
√ Keep the focus on the person presenting (don't switch to your issues).
√ Ask open-ended questions or offer non-judgmental observations ...
√ Be attentive to patterns of responses; pause to allow quieter ones to speak.

(For a book review or an original paper, responses may vary from those above.)

BREAK (5 MINUTES)

SECOND PRESENTATION (50 MINUTES)

Process the meeting (5 minutes).

√ How well did the group stay focused on the presenter (let each answer)?

√ How was the ratio of critique and affirmation?

√ How open and prayerful was the group? Were there times it was too fast-paced?

CLOSURE: Choose a ritual of closure, or one that the leader suggests. Examples:

1. Chant or sing, offer a poem or scripture or say the Serenity Prayer.
2. Invite each to turn left palm up, right palm down; in silence join hands as a symbol of receiving (left) and giving (right).
3. Join right hands in center (like spokes in a wheel), then place left hand on shoulder of person on left (in silence or with spoken blessing).
4. Pass around a stone, candle or other object, in silence (Variation: This can be done during opening as well, using the object as a "talking stick," then passing it to next person who shares.)
5. Offer a single sentence blessing (or in silence) for the person on your right, followed "Amen"—as the cue for the next person.

Resource Three: Creating a Life Mission Statement

Meditate with Frederick Buechner's words in *Wishful Thinking*: "The place God calls you to is the place where your deep gladness and the world's deep hunger meets."[48]

On a clean page in your journal or a new document in your computer write: *I am here on this earth to...* Let your mission statement reflect this two-fold focus: What puts a sparkle in your eyes? (your deep gladness) and What pulls at your heartstrings? (some deep hunger of the world). Avoid being too generic (to love everyone) or too specific (to lay bricks). Put your flesh on your mission with the words *through* or *by*: "to express love through the building blocks of my life, or by creating..."

For a youth your mission can guide you for decades to come; for an elder it can flood past decades with meaning. Word it in a way that speaks to employment or retirement or disability. Rework your mission; keep it short; repeat is as a prayer of your heart; put it on a card inside your closet or desk or wallet.

Idea: Reread the opening stem: *I am here on this earth to...* Pause for a couple of minutes with this phrase as your heart's prayer, to be present to your self and God and the world. Begin to write. When you stop, read what you've written once; then a second time highlight or underline phrases that leap out at you. Condense the highlights to one vital sentence. (Incorporate other aspects as goals or objectives.)

Option: Art Your Life Mission. Let an image or metaphor arise that encapsulates the essence of your life mission. Experiment with a non-linear way to express it in art... chalk... pastels... clay... poetry... music... or movement.

Bibliography

SPIRITUAL PRACTICES AND VOCATION

Bolles, Richard. *What Color Is Your Parachute? A Practical Manual for Job-Hunters and Career-Changers* (Berkeley: Ten Speed Press, 2011).

Epperly, Bruce G. and Katherine Gould Epperly. *Tending the Holy: The Practice of the Presence of God in Ministry.* (Herndon, Virginia: The Alban Institute, 2009).

Groff, Kent Ira. *Writing Tides: Finding Grace and Growth through Writing.* (Nashville: Abingdon Press, 2007).

Jones, Lori Beth. *The Path: Creating Your Mission Statement for Work and for Life* (New York: Hyperion, 1996).

May, Gerald G., M.D. *Addiction and Grace.* (San Francisco: Harper & Row, 1988).

de Mello, Anthony. *Sadhana: A Way to God: Christian Exercises in Eastern Form.* (New York: Doubleday, 1978, 1984).

Paintner, Christine Valters, Ph.D. *Lectio Divina—The Sacred Art: Transforming Words and Images into Heart-Centered Prayer.* (Woodstock, Vermont: Skylight Paths, 2011).

Palmer, Parker J. *A Hidden Wholeness: The Journey Toward an Undivided Life.* (San Francisco: Jossey-Bass, 2004).

Eugene Peterson, *The Pastor: A Memoir.* (New York: HarperOne, 2011).

Evelyn Underhill, *The Spiritual Life.* (Harrisburg, Pennsylvania: Morehouse Publishing, 1999).

CHANGING PERSPECTIVES ON CHURCH AND SPIRITUALITY

Borg, Marcus J. and John Dominic Crossan. *The First Christmas: What the Gospels Really Teach about Jesus's Birth.* (San Francisco: HarperOne, 2007).

Borg, Marcus J. and N. T. Wright. *The Meaning of Jesus: Two Visions.* (San Francisco: HarperSanFrancisco, 1999).

Groff, Kent Ira. *What Would I Believe If I Didn't Believe Anything?: A Handbook for Spiritual Orphans.* (San Francisco: Jossey-Bass, 2004).

Hanh, Thich Nhat. *Living Buddha, Living Christ.* (New York: Riverhead Books, 1995).

McLaren, Brian D. *A New Kind of Christianity: Ten Questions That Are Transforming the Faith.* (San Francisco: HarperOne, 2010).

Spong, John Shelby. *A New Christianity for a New World: Why Traditional Faith is Dying and How a New Faith Is Being Born.* (San Francisco: HarperSanFrancisco, 2002).

GENERATIONAL ISSUES IN WORK AND MINISTRY

Merritt, Carol Howard, *Tribal Church: Ministering to the Missing Generation.* (Herndon, Virginia: The Alban Institute, 2007).

Lancaster, Lynne and David Stillman, *When Generations Collide.* (New York: Collins Business, 2005).

Parks, Sharon Daloz. *Big Questions, Worthy Dreams: Mentoring Young Adults in Their Search for Meaning, Purpose, and Faith.* (San Francisco: Jossey-Bass, 2001).

Sutherland, Anne. *Claiming the Beatitudes: Nine Stories from a New Generation.* (Herndon, Virginia: The Alban Institute, 2009).

Sweeney, Jon M., ed. *God Within: Our Spiritual Future—As Told by Today's New Adults.* (Woodstock, Vermont: Skylight Paths, 2001).

Endnotes

1. Ernest Kurtz and Katherine Ketcham, *The Spirituality of Imperfection* (New York: Bantam Books, 1992), 153.
2. Grenaé D. Dudley and Carlyle Fielding Stewart, III, *Sankofa: Celebrations for the African American Church* (Cleveland: United Church Press, 1997), 9.
3. This examen is adapted from Ignatius of Loyola's *Spiritual Exercises*. For my fuller summary, see *Facing East, Praying West* (New York: Paulist Press, 2010), 5.
4. Robert K. Greenleaf, *Servant Leadership: A Journey into the Nature of Legitimate Power and Greatness* (New York: Paulist Press, 1977), 239, italics original.
5. *The New Millennium Spiritual Journey* by the editors of Skylight Paths (Woodstock, Vermont: Skylight Paths Publishing, 1999), 21.
6. Thomas Merton, *The Seven Storey Mountain* (New York: Harcourt Brace Jovanovich, 1945; 1976), p. 414.
7. *Alcoholics Anonymous: The Story of How Thousands of Men and Women Have Recovered*, the so-called "AA Big Book," 87-88. (New York: AA World Services, Inc., 2001), 87-88.
8. See Christine Valters Paintner, Ph.D, *Lectio Divina—The Sacred Art: Transforming Words and Images into Heart-Centered Prayer* (Woodstock, Vermont: Skylight Paths, 2011).
9. Thomas Merton, *New Seeds of Contemplation* (New York: New Directions Paperbook, 1972), 14.
10. John H. Timmerman, "In Search of the Great Goodness: The Poetry of Jane Kenyon," in *Perspectives* (May 2003). See also Timmerman's *Jane Kenyon: A Literary Life* (Grand Rapids: Eerdman's 2002).
11. Helen Keller, *Light in My Darkness*, rev. and ed. by Ray Silverman (West Chester, Pennsylvania: Chrysalis Books, 1994), 21.
12. Trevor Farrell, with his wife and other young adults, was interviewed on Public Radio Saturday, January 27, 2006.
13. Sharon Daloz Parks, *Big Questions, Worthy Dreams: Mentoring Young Adults in Their Search for Meaning, Purpose, and Faith* (San Francisco: Jossey-Bass Inc., 2000), 137-38.
14. Mary Oliver, *House of Light* (Boston: Beacon Press, 1990), 57.
15. Zora Neale Hurston. *Their Eyes Were Watching God* (New York: HarperPerennial, 1990), 21.
16. Garth Stein, *The Art of Racing in the Rain: A Novel* (New York: Harper, 2008), p. 101-102.

17. "Young and Bipolar" by Jeffrey Kluger with Sora Song is the feature article in *Time* August 19, 2002 (Vol. 160, No. 8), 38-47

18. John Keats, quoted by Christopher Bamford in "Negative Capability," *Parabola* (May 2005, Vol. 30, No. 2), 15-16.

19. In Wayne Muller, *Sabbaths* (New York: Bantam Books, 1999), 190.

20. The Shawshank Redemption quote is taken from Edward McNulty, *Praying the Movies* (Louisville: Geneva Press, 2001), 59.

21. Andrew Solomon, *The Noonday Demon: An Atlas of Depression* (New York: Scribner, 2001), pp. 16-17.

22. *Space for God* is the title of an excellent book for personal or group study and prayer, by Don Postema (Grand Rapids: CRC Publications, 1983).

23. Evelyn Underhill, *The Spiritual Life* (Harrisburg, Pennsylvania: Morehouse Publishing, 1999), 55.

24. Kent Ira Groff, "Seven Spiritual Strategies for Pastoral Conflict," *Congregations: The Alban Journal,* XXIII: 6, 1997.

25. See "Choosing Well, Living Whole" in Kent Ira Groff, *Facing East, Praying West: Poetic Reflections on The Spiritual Exercises* (New York: Paulist Press, 2010), 55-56.

26. http://www.couragerenewal.org/parker/writings/clearness-committee

27. Lynn C. Lancaster and David Stillman, *When Generations Collide: Who They Are. Why They Clash. How to Solve the Generational Puzzle at Work* (New York: CollinsBusiness, 2005), 319-20.

28. Mencius IV.B.12, "Confucianism" in *World Scripture: A Comparative Anthology of Sacred Texts,* ed. by Andrew Wilson (St. Paul: Paragon House, 1995), 144.

29. John 3:3-5.

30. *The Gift: Poems by Hafiz the Great Sufi Master* translated by Daniel Ladinsky (New York: Penguin Compass, 1999), 107.

31. Margaret Geller, "The Sense of Wonder," Literary Exercises of Phi Beta Kappa, Harvard Commencement, June 1995. http://gos.sbc.edu/g/geller.html

32. Richard Restak, M.D., *Mozart's Brain and the Fighter Pilot: Unleashing Your Brain's Potential* (New York: Three Rivers Press, 2001), 181.

33. Quoted from Mark Sundby and Susan Nienaber, "The Pastor and Pornography," (The Alban Institute): www.alban.org/conversation.aspx?id=9728

34. The quote is adapted from "Out of Ur": www.outofur.com/archives/2006/08/word_for_word_w.html

35. Quoted from Mark Sundby and Susan Nienaber, "The Pastor and Pornography," (The Alban Institute, 2011): www.alban.org/conversation.aspx?id=9728

36. The Alban authors refer to *Newsweek* (Vol. 158, Issue 4), 61.

37. Gerald G. May, M.D., *Addiction and Grace* (San Francisco: Harper & Row, 1988), pp. 91; 139, italics in original.

38. I heard Arun Gandhi tell this story at the American Academy of Religion in Toronto, Ontario, November 18, 2002 and at Chautauqua Institution, New York, July 7, 2006.

39. Brian R. Greene, *The Elegant Universe: Superstrings, Hidden Dimensions, and the Quest for the Ultimate Theory* (New York: W.W. Norton, 1999), 15.

40. The phrase high-tech/high-touch comes from John Naisbitt's *Megatrends* (New York: Warner Books, 1982).

41. Story from John Shelby Spong, "Jesus for the 21st Century," lectures at Chautauqua Institution, N.Y., July 12-13, 2000.

42. Ricoeur's phrase is quoted in James W. Fowler, *Stages of Faith: The Psychology of Human Development and the Quest for Meaning* (San Francisco: HarperSanfrancisco, 1995), 187-88 and 197.

43. T.S. Eliot, "The Dry Salvages" from *Four Quartets* (New York: Harcourt Brace & Co., 1943), 44.

44. I have slightly adapted the English translation of Albert Schweitzer's German in his concluding paragraph of *The Quest of the Historical Jesus* (Baltimore: Johns Hopkins University Press, 1998), 403.

45. C. S. Lewis, *Mere Christianity* (New York: The Macmillan Company, 1958), ix.

46. The story of Bud and Hope church is summarized from Thomas R. Hawkins, *The Learning Congregation* (Louisville: Westminster John Knox Press, 1997), 131.

47. This story of the Atheist Coalition meeting on Easter is told by John Galloway, a Presbyterian minister in Wayne, Pennsylvania.

48. Frederick Buechner, *Wishful Thinking: A Theological ABC* (San Francisco: Harper & Row, 1973), 95.

Also by APC Authors
from Energion Publications

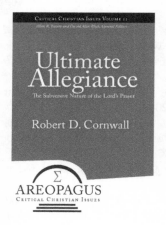

AREOPAGUS
CRITICAL CHRISTIAN ISSUES

The most recited prayer is performed more often than it is prayed. Bob Cornwall thoughtfully challenges us to recognize the subversive nature of the words we speak. When we truly pray the Lord's Prayer, God pushes us to worship deeply, live bravely, trust fully, forgive freely, and celebrate joyfully. This book is for those who are willing to honestly question their ultimate allegiance.

Brett Younger
Associate Professor of Preaching
McAfee School of Theology, Atlanta

This is a serious book about a subject we focus on all too seldom these days — the power and the meaning of the Cross of Christ. I'm glad to say it warmed my heart. I think it will warm yours as well.

John Killinger
Professor, pastor, and author of 50 books, including *The Changing Shape of Our Salvation*

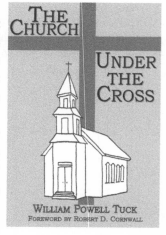

More from Energion Publications

Personal Study

Finding My Way in Christianity	Herold Weiss	$16.99
When People Speak for God	Henry Neufeld	$17.99

Church and Ministry

Crossing the Street	Robert LaRochelle, APC	$17.99
Out of This World	Darren M. McClellan	$24.99

Bible Study

Learning and Living Scripture	Lentz & Neufeld	$12.99
Philippians: A Participatory Study Guide	Bruce Epperly	$9.99
Ephesians: A Participatory Study Guide	Bob Cornwall, APC	$9.99

Theology

The Church Under the Cross	William Powell Tuck, FAPC	$11.99
From Inspiration to Understanding	Edward W. H. Vick	$24.99
Creation: The Christian Doctrine	Edward W. H. Vick	$12.99
Creation in Scripture	Herold Weiss	$12.99
Ultimate Allegiance	Bob Cornwall, APC	$9.99

Forthcoming

Healing Marks	Bruce Epperly
Transforming Acts: Mysticism and Mission in a Pluralistic Age	Bruce Epperly

Generous Quantity Discounts Available
Dealer Inquiries Welcome
Energion Publications
P.O. Box 841
Gonzalez, FL 32560
Website: http://energionpubs.com
Phone: (850) 525-3916